Comedia Series ● No. 24

TELEVISION MYTHOLOGIES:
STARS, SHOWS & SIGNS

Edited by Len Masterman

Comedia Publishing Group/MK Media Press
9 Poland Street, London WIV 3DG   Tel: 01-439 2059
In association with Marion Boyars, London and New York
24 Lacy Road, London SW15 & 262 West 22nd Street, New York

Comedia Publishing Group was set up to investigate and monitor the media in Britain and abroad. The aim of the project is to provide basic information and analysis, to investigate problem areas, and to encourage debate about the future of the media. The opinions expressed in the book are those of the authors, and do not necessarily reflect the views of Comedia.

For a list of other Comedia titles see page 141.

ISBN 0 906 890 56X (paperback)
ISBN 0 906 890 551 (hardback)

British Library Cataloguing in Publication Data

Masterman, Len
Television mythologies
1. Television programs
I. Title
   791.45'75   PN1992.5

Cover design by Andrew Whittle

Typeset by Photosetting, 6 Foundry House,
Stars Lane, Yeovil, Somerset BA20 1NL

Printed by Unwin Brothers Ltd
The Gresham Press, Old Woking, Surrey

Trade distribution by Marion Boyars
24 Lacy Road London S.W.15

Distributed in USA by Marion Boyars
and The Scribner Book Companies

Distributed in Australia by Second Back Row Press
50 Govett Street, Katoomba, N.S.W. 2780

Contents

TELEVISION MYTHOLOGIES: Stars, Shows and Signs

Introduction – Len Masterman   1

1. All in the Family: Russell Grant on Breakfast Television – *Elizabeth Wilson*   7

2. That's Life – *Robin Gutch*   10

3. One Man and his Dog Show – *Philip Simpson*   16

4. What's My Line? – *Rosalind Brunt*   21

5. All in Fun: Su Pollard on Disney Time – *Cary Bazalgette*   29

6. Black Blue Peter – *Bob Ferguson*   34

7. TV Games: People as Performers – *Bill Lewis*   42

8. Top of the Pops: the Politics of the Living Room – *Sean Cubitt*   46

9. Fragments of Neil: Entertainment & Political Leadership – *Richard Paterson*   49

10. Romantic Perfection: the Torvill & Dean Story – *Bruce Carson*   54

11. Olympic Myths: the Flame, the Night & the Music – *John Corner*   58

12. TV Commercials: Moving Statues and Old Movies – *Colin McArthur*   63

13. 'She laughed at me with my own teeth': Tommy Cooper – Television Anti-Hero – *Albert Hunt*   67

14. The Glut of the Personality – *David Lusted*   73

15. Writing about Soap Opera – *Charlotte Brunsdon*   82

16. Fabulous Powers: Blaming the Media – *Ian Connell*   88

17. The 'A' Team: Paradigms of Masculinity – *David Widgery*   94

18. The Battle of Orgreave – *Len Masterman*   99

19. Today's Television and Tomorrow's World –
    Frank Webster & Kevin Robins   110

20. TV Magazines: Workers' Profiles? –
    John O. Thompson   114

21. Out of Bounds: the Myth of Marginality – *John Hartley*   118

22. Disembodied Voices & Familiar Faces: Television
    Continuity – *Ed Buscombe*   128

23. Television Previewers: No Critical Comment – *Kathy Myers* 132

    List of contributors   139

Dedication

In living memory of Roland Barthes, who understood that a critic needs also to be a fan.

Acknowledgments

To David Morley for detailed editorial assistance which has extended well beyond the normal duties of publisher. The expeditious completion of this project is entirely his achievement.

Thanks to the Nottingham English and Politics Group for their sustained assistance and dialogue over the past two years.

L.M.

Introduction

Roland Barthes wrote *Mythologies* between 1954 and 1956. His sharp and elegant studies of such aspects of popular culture as striptease, wrestling, toys, tourist guides, etc., were produced at a time when most of the contributors to this volume were still at school. Such is the insularity of British culture that *Mythologies* was not translated into English until 1972. It made an immediate impact. Dated and removed from British cultural interests though its subject matter frequently was, it nevertheless spoke vigorously and directly to many people who had for some time been questioning the eternal verities of British literary culture. Among the verities in question were the assertion of the pre-eminent significance of literature, the concomitant devaluation of popular cultural forms and the displacement of political and ideological questions into questions of literary value.

Mythologies turned these values upside down. Firstly, Barthes published his pieces not in academic journals, but in popular magazines. And the sharpest possible rejection of established tastes was implicit in his choice of subject. If a plate of steak and chips, a margarine advertisement and a poem were to be seen as equally worthy of serious critical attention, then a significant step had been taken towards a truly scandalous *equation* between these objects.

To the horror of the traditionalists there did not seem to be any process of discriminatory filtering in Barthes' selection of some subjects rather than others. Indeed, topics appeared to be chosen at random, as they were suggested by current events. Implicit in Barthes' very methodology was an undermining of the bedrock distinctions between cultural objects, and between the qualities and values supposedly inherent within them, upon which literary study itself had been constituted.

Significantly too *Mythologies* offered a direct challenge to those absolute distinctions, which still have considerable force within British culture, between politics and other cultural spheres, such as literature, education or sport. Within 'English' this spiriting away of politics from literary culture has been a key element in the historical development of the subject. Indeed, English can be seen to owe both its origins as an academic subject, and its increasing institutionalisation in schools and universities, to its perceived role as a powerful counterbalance to the threat of serious social disruption. The bracketing off of politics from literature was no historical accident. It was endemic to the origins of the whole English project. Matthew Arnold's *Culture and Anarchy*, for example, was a response to the 'breakdown' of law-and-order provoked by the 1866 suffrage demonstrations. Arnoldian 'Culture', with literature as its fulcrum, was called into being as an ideological bulwark against working-class political activism, and the extension of the franchise.

The importance of English in domesticating the working classes, both by initiating them into the national culture and transmitting to them 'moral values' led, in the twentieth century, to its increasing centrality in the development of the national education system. At the end of the Great War the spectre of Bolshevism, the collapse of Liberalism at home and the decline of religion, provoked fears of serious social upheaval. One of the most influential educational documents of the time, the Newbolt Report on *The Teaching of English in England* (1921), had no doubts about the importance of English in meeting these social and ideological challenges.

'We were told that the working classes, especially those belonging to organised labour movements, were antagonistic to, and con-temptuous of, literature... Literature... as a subject of instruction is suspect as an attempt to "side-track the working-class movement". We regard the prevalence of such opinions as a serious matter... chiefly because it points to a morbid condition of the body politic which, if not taken in hand, may be followed by lamentable consequences. For if literature be... a fellowship which 'binds together by passion and knowledge the vast empire of human society, as it is spread over the whole earth and over all time" then the nation of which a considerable portion rejects this means of grace and despises this great spiritual influence must assuredly be heading for disaster.'

George Sampson, himself a member of the Newbolt Committee, made the point most explicitly of all in his book, *English for the English* (1926):

'Deny to working-class children any common share in the im-material, and presently they will grow into the men who demand with menaces a communism of the material.'

In the 1930s and '40s the work of F. R. Leavis and the literary quarterly *Scrutiny* completed this extended project of staking out the ground for literary culture as the repository of spiritual and moral values, above and beyond politics. In a period of prolonged political crisis, which saw the emergence of the Labour Party as a powerful force in British politics, it is curious that what should re-emerge as a contender for cultural hegemony was Arnoldianism, one of whose principal effects was, in Francis Mulhern's words

'a *depreciation*, a *repression*, and at the limit, a *categorical dissolution of politics as such.*'

In relation to the media, Leavisism forestalled for two generations any serious consideration within British culture of their ideological role, of their function as consciousness industries. What it put in their place was a theory of literary value and, in particular, an emphasis upon the importance of critical discrimination ('the sense that this is worth more than that') which persists as a limiting factor in discussions about the media down to the present day.

Mythologies cut decisively through these carefully constituted historical distinctions between politics and culture and asserted the necessity of understanding the political in its widest sense as describing 'the whole of human relations in their real, social structure, in their power of making the world'. What *Mythologies* demonstrated was the *centrality of power relations* – of patterns of dominance, oppression and subordination – to the process of signification. The book took a significant step towards demystifying literature as a privileged mode of cultural practice. After *Mythologies* it became increasingly difficult to keep the ideological constitution of the field of 'English' – the power relations inscribed within the processes of selecting, ordering, evaluating and ranking particular kinds of writing – off the agenda.

If *Mythologies* were shocking and subversive to established interests, to many teachers it was a heady, exhilarating brew. To be autobiographical for a moment, in 1972 I had begun to teach a Television Studies course in school, as a way of responding to my hardening conviction (a conviction forced upon me above all by the reactions of my students) that middle-class cultural values, forms and language had little to offer students within multi-cultural and predominantly working-class classrooms. My television teaching at least allowed me to acknowledge the importance of the students' own cultural experiences and enabled me to raise a host of important ideological, conceptual and pedagogic questions which had long been repressed by literary studies. *Mythologies* was published just after I began my teaching. Like many others, I was immediately attracted by its generosity of spirit, and its openness to all aspects of culture, which revealingly highlighted, by contrast, the besetting exclusivity of Anglo-American writing about both established and popular culture. Of immediate psychological and practical value, too, were its confident, unapologetic tone, its centring of ideological questions and its systematic search for a critical methodology. But most helpful of all, standing at the heart of *Mythologies*, and not simply eschewing bourgeois culture, but revealing it as *the* problem, lay the key to a new way of conceptualising experience: Barthes' notion of Myth.

Myth, for Barthes, was a mode of representation, 'a kind of speech', characterised above all by its 'self-evident truth', its 'naturalness'. The origin of *Mythologies* lay in Barthes' rejection of the way in which newspapers, magazines, films and exhibitions represented social constructions – the outcome of historical and political struggles – as simply 'natural' or common-sense:

'The starting point of these reflections was usually a feeling of impatience at the sight of the "naturalness" with which newspapers, art and common sense constantly dress up a reality which, even though it is the one we live in, is undoubtedly determined by history. In short, in the account given of our contemporary circumstances, I resented seeing Nature and History confused at every turn, and I wanted to track down, in the decorative display of *what-goes-without-saying*, the ideological abuse which, in my view, is hidden there'

(Preface to Mythologies*)*

For Barthes, the production of myths is conditional upon two, linked repressions: of history and of politics. The 'transformation' of History into Nature was, for Barthes, 'the very principle of Myth':

'Myth deprives the object of which it speaks of all History. In it history evaporates. It is a kind of ideal servant: it prepares all things, brings them, lays them out, the master arrives, it silently disappears: all that is left for one to do is to enjoy this beautiful object without wondering where it comes from. Or even better it can only come from eternity: since the beginning of time, it has been made for bourgeois man . . Nothing is produced, nothing is chosen: all one has to do is to possess these new objects, from which all soiling trace of origin or choice has been removed. This miraculous evaporation of history is another form of a concept common to most bourgeois myths: the irresponsibility of man.'

('Myth Today', Mythologies*)*

In denying history, Myth also denies politics: *'Myth is depoliticised speech'*. What Myth 'forgets' is that reality is forged dialectically, that it is a product of human activity and struggle. This is why Barthes describes the function of Myth as being 'to empty reality; it is literally a ceaseless flowing out, a haemorrhage, or perhaps an evaporation, in short a perceptible absence'. And, as history, politics and struggle flow out, during the process of representation, Nature, unchanging, and unchangeable, floods in. The task of cultural criticism, for Barthes, was to reverse that flow, to challenge the undialectical and

common-sensed representations of the media, through a criticism
which restored the history, the politics and the struggle to those
representations.

Barthes' notion of Myth was formulated as a result of his
reflections upon pre-television media. Yet television, constantly
denying its own mode of production, continually manufacturing for
its audiences a seamless, plausible and authentic flow of 'natural'
images, easily outdoes all other media in its effortless production of
cultural myths, 'realities' which go-without-saying. Uncovering such
myths ought to be an important objective for any television criticism.
We need to demonstrate precisely how and why television's
representations are produced – by whom, in whose interests, using
what kind of rhetorical techniques, and producing what kind of
consciousness – rather than simply accepting them as 'reflections',
part of the way-things-are. Television criticism as presently constituted in the press and on television itself, however, is constructed
either as a relatively marginal, somewhat trivial pursuit (as in the
popular tabloids or BBC's *Points of View* programme) or as a matter
of individual sensibility (the 'quality' press and BBC 2's *Did You
See?*). At all levels it operates under a disabling tension. The impulse
to articulate feelings and opinions about *quality* is constantly under-
mined by the difficulty of establishing any widely agreed judgemental
criteria which would underpin them.

A programme like *Did You See?* solves this problem by
suspending itself uneasily between two dominant bourgeois views of
the medium. On the one hand a window-on-the-world view of
television is implicit in the selection of many of the guest critics who
are chosen for their expertise in relation to the *content* of a particular
programme (football manager, Lawrie McMenemy, criticising *Match
of the Day*, for example).

On the other hand, television becomes an arena for the display of
bourgeois sensibility, and other critics are chosen because they
belong to that minority for whom, irrespective of their knowledge of
television, or even of programme content, feeling *is* judgement. So,
composer-writer Tim Rice, for example, can be asked his opinion of
soap opera, even though he confesses to never having seen *Coronation
Street*. Typically in *Did You See?* the sensibilities which play upon
television have been nurtured within the traditional arts. What the
show celebrates is not television but the notion of the critic as unique
individual. Yet, paradoxically, the critic must be established as more
than merely idiosyncratic. The unspoken assumption of all criticism
is that it is, in some sense, *representative*, that it strikes *some* chord in
its audience. But, in the case of *Did You See?*, of what is it
representative? Of that untheorised abstraction 'the viewing aud-

ience"? Hardly. Of a disciplined, coherently constituted and well-established television criticism? Such a criticism is scarcely likely to be found in a practice which is predominantly dismissive of television (and here Rice's reaction is quite typical). What is represented in the programme, rather, occupying uncertain ground somewhere between the pretentiousness of the 'posh' Sundays' arts reviews, and the vagaries of wine-tasting, is a wholly implicit and thoroughly discredited bourgeois notion of 'taste'. Its authority derives not from any conceptual coherence, but from its assertion by a particular fraction of a social class powerful and confident enough to elevate its personal preferences to the status of judgements of 'quality'.

This collection of essays testifies to the existence of a sturdy and quite different strain of cultural criticism within Britain, which has been almost entirely unrecorded by the media themselves, but which deserves far wider attention than it has so far received. Written during the summer of 1984, these essays represent a collaborative attempt to unearth some of the myths perpetuated by British television during that period. Public debates and private conversations about the media generally take place within the limited paradigms set by dominant media 'criticism'. The development of a public opinion which *counts* in the field of television (as it does, say, on nuclear issues), because it is well-informed, broadly based, and asks the right kind of questions, is a matter of urgent necessity. Those with power and authority still manage to have too much untrammelled success for the good of democracy in manufacturing an unspoken form of consent for *their* ways of seeing via television.

So, this volume is intended both as an *homage* to Roland Barthes, and as a contribution to the long struggle to make the serious consideration of television's ideological role part of the accepted currency of public debate about the medium. In this spirit, readers' comments on this collection will be warmly received, as will any analyses of programmes which readers may care to submit for consideration for future publications.

Len Masterman,
Nottingham,
October, 1984

Elizabeth Wilson

All in the Family:
Russell Grant on Breakfast Television

The strange thing about the *Breakfast Time* family is the absence of Mother. Father (Frank) and daughter (Selina) keep the wheels turning smoothly and there are other young and invariably personable men and women to maintain the atmosphere of slightly manic, Home Counties cheerfulness. Is it an extended family, or a children's home for adolescents? Its compulsive domesticity, its relentless banality are what make it so modern – the normalizing of the abnormal is what it's all about.

The living room in which the cosy in-jokes are bandied about has as much individuality as those 'Rooms of My Own' of which we read every week in the colour supplement, 'designed for me/us by So and So' – everything's too new and too bright. Indeed, the normality is such that it borders on the mad. It reminds me of the coffee shoppe at the Los Angeles Greyhound Terminal. A fairly large number of homeless persons appear actually to live in the Terminal, and the coffee shoppe was designed presumably with them in mind, since it is in fact decorated to look like a living room, with fake shelves of books, pictures, vases of plastic flowers, a chimney piece with an old-fashioned coffee pot perched upon it; while the only slightly discordant note is a bicycle suspended against the wall. Still, some families *do* hang their bicycles up on walls. The *Breakfast Time* living room reminds me a little of that determinedly cheerful, over-bright coffee shoppe in downtown L.A.

Equally, the façade of familial normality disguises the fact that what we are dealing with is a group of non-related individuals pretending to be a family – just like a local authority children's home. Just as in a modern, trendy children's home, there's a big emphasis on Entertainment. All concerned cheerfully look on The Positive, and keep their sense of humour intact. Frank's avuncularity and senior social worker casual wear makes us all feel safe – he knows how to Set Limits, and he'd be the one to get the kids all playing 'I Spy' in the fall-out shelter. Like all Housefathers (not that they're called that any more), though, *he*'s slightly odd as well, because although he's paternalism personified, his woolly gives the game away: he's wearing what Dads wear at home when they're *not at work*; and yet – he *is* at work. This is his work – pretending to be Daddy on *Breakfast Time*. So, like all housefathers, his heartiness is a tiny bit phoney.

He incarnates the modern, liberal, Life-as-Therapeutic-Enterprise view of the family: that everything is really a family – households of friends, homosexual lovers, even the institutionalized in prisons and hospitals, all are *really* a kind of family. And as in all good families, nothing bad can ever really happen. So there isn't much news on *Breakfast Time*. There is some, of course, reality can't be entirely avoided, but most mornings viewers need hardly notice it because the news is largely reduced to gossip by the tidal wave of gossip that surrounds and submerges it. Traffic news and weather is one sort of gossip; what's happening on the South Circular? They say there's a terrible hold-up. Are the Southern Region trains late *again*? It's those Unions! Where's the Green Goddess today? (Livening up old age pensioners in Humberside or sorting out the Town Hall admin. staff of Slough in Berkshire). Recipes, titbits of fashion news, reports from the pop charts or the football field – all these are the media version of family gossip.

All in all, *Breakfast Time* attempts – and succeeds in – the heroic enterprise of creating a cosy sense of family normality out of the least amenable material: world news and current affairs are miraculously transformed into a family soap opera. It also makes clear how inescapably middle-class is this style of the normalization of daily life. Precisely the madness of the petit bourgeois consciousness is its ability to make the craziest and most terrifying events appear banal.

What, in that case, is Russell Grant of all people doing in this cosy family set-up? Plump, outrageously camp, and daringly dressed, he cannot – *surely* – be said to conform to any standards of family normality.

Unlike the rest of the family, who have to keep the whole thing going for the full three hours or so of its daily life, Russell Grant appears only once daily on the programme – at the shockingly late hour of 8.40. Russell is always treated like a star. Shamelessly he boasts, shows off and upstages the adults. Once, when wearing a kind of loose, caftan-type shirt, he lifted its hem with infant naughtiness – just like a little four-year-old girl showing her knickers to Daddy – to reveal: his tummy. He's allowed that kind of behaviour, because at that age they don't quite realise what they're doing, do they?

If the programme as a whole tends towards the mildly manic, with Russell's appearance the mania reaches screaming point. He exploits to the full the brutal cheerfulness of camp, which simultaneously tramples the victim's feelings (but the victim is the subject as well as the object of his jokes) and makes that same victim somehow feel important.

And Russell certainly makes the viewers feel important. Through Russell's agency the whole nation can become part of the *Breakfast Time* happy family. All across the nation, from Ilfracombe to Aberdeen, the great extended family of his fan clubs send their letters, special cards and – of course – snapshots. And Russell loves them all to pieces, beams out his thanks and seems to speak to each and every one of us via the medium of the Horoscope. ('Now listen, all you naughty Taureans...') He reads out our Fate of the Day in a whirlwind of expectation ('Hold on to your hats..') And we can think about our anxieties, yet maintain that vital Sense of Humour without which the whole edifice would collapse.

And as he swans in and out of the programme, like a nouveau riche auntie in a cloud of Californian Poppy, it is clear that he too – even he – is, after all, just as much part of the family as everyone else. Somehow he's the rich, vulgar auntie and her spoilt little Violet Elizabeth – or even William himself – at one and the same time.

He's the vulgar outsider who exists in every family – the one whose outrage reinforces the rest of us in our sense of our normality; the grand eccentric who acts out the rudeness in which we'd all like to indulge; the show-off in the most stiff upper-lipped of us; the child in every adult. If you dared to cross him, the sunny smile would change into temper tantrum, he'd soon tell Auntie if you took one of the sweets he's cramming into his mouth. He's the spoilt child in every home, the family tyrant, the unacceptable face of kinship, His Majesty the Baby.

He needs a mother's hand – then everything would have been different. But where *is* Mother? Uncle Frank won't say – but Selina always was his favourite daughter.

Robin Gutch

That's Life

'Life throws at us a mixture of farce and tragedy and if you're going to do a programme about people's real lives you ought to include both extremes. One minute a talking dog, then perhaps cot design faults causing babies' deaths in Spanish hotels the next. That's Life.'

(Esther Rantzen, Radio Times *3.1.81)*

Few of us own talking dogs or, fortunately, have had our children die in the cots of Spanish hotels. Yet both are apparently true of our 'real' lives. A banal truism blends with patent absurdity to produce a statement which can only be meaningful within the terms of a mythology claiming to encompass *all* the multitudinous phenomena of human experience. A mythology which reduces History to a series of banana-skins strewn in our biographical paths by a negligent Destiny.

That's Life developed out of *Braden's Week*, another popular consumer programme, in 1973. The self-conscious formula of addressing the frustrations of everyday experience within the framework of a popular culture largely ignored by 'factual' television has made *That's Life* not only enormously popular (peaking with 20 million viewers in 1981), but also television's recognised champion of the people. "I love the way she takes on authority. The ordinary person gets nowhere. Esther gets results." (*Sunday People*, 22.1.84). This populist status has been achieved through the deployment of specific television conventions and an exploitation of the traditions of urban working-class culture, successfully constructing a distinctive *That's Life* mythology.

During its eleven-year history *That's Life* has evolved into a textual hybrid which uniquely combines the conventions of current affairs and variety light entertainment television. Produced by the BBC Current Affairs Department, it is transmitted almost immediately after the recording, thus invoking the myth of 'live' broadcasting. The presenters speak direct to camera sitting at newsdesks, while there are films from reporters who report back to the studio about the 'real world out there'. The programme's discourse is thus seen to be referring to the same 'reality' brought to us daily by current affairs television.

But *That's Life* is also constructed as a variety 'show' to be performed in front of an audience, beginning in traditional style with Rantzen and (at a suitably deferent distance) the 'team' coming on set to audience applause. The show progresses through the mediating presence of Rantzen as 'star', often involving interaction between her, team and audience with frequent 'double entendres'. Together with the 'star guest appearances' of 'ordinary people', the recording of audience reaction over the films, and 'soft' lighting and design, these conventions combine to designate *That's Life* as 'entertainment', where the 'real' can be incorporated into the world of 'play'.

Consequently the specific discourse of *That's Life* operates through an interplay between conventions which simultaneously constructs a 'real' world and a 'play' world for the audience. Far from opposing the two (as did the old *Nationwide*'s skateboarding duck/the Budget type of opposition) this discourse constructs the two worlds as being effectively the same – the *That's Life* world of 'tragedy and farce'. This mythological world is given its distinctive identity through the re-packaging of themes drawn from traditional British popular culture.

The brass band *That's Life* theme music, reinforced by the closing credit graphics (which stylistically allude to traditional seaside postcards), indicates the programme's concern to represent itself as part of a continuous popular tradition. Yet it studiously avoids references to contemporary popular culture, such as youth sub-cultures or the mass media. Despite being a consumer programme, *That's Life* paradoxically appeals to the values of a mythological pre-consumerist culture evoked in programmes such as *Coronation Street*.

This is most apparent in *That's Life*'s treatment of sexuality. Remarkably for a BBC 1 programme on Sunday night, there are continual references to the sexual and bodily functions normally repressed from the (non-fictional) discourses of television. The notorious vegetables and Cyril's Odes have been replaced by the 'Newsdesk' of Doc Cox and Joanna Munro, who present a selection of the newspaper cuttings and photographs viewers have sent in. Almost invariably these demonstrate the impromptu appearance of references to the sexual or excretory in some form of 'official' discourse, whether from impersonal printed newspapers or the insignia of officialdom, such as car numberplates or noticeboards: 'two pairs of inter-copulating bedrooms', 'a supplement of £35 per person per wee', a numberplate on a Jaguar spelling BUL 54IT, a caption reading 'a group of queens' beside a picture of local dignitaries.

This compulsive process reproduces the humour of the popular

Carry On films. Both offer the pleasure of our animal instinctive natures triumphing over the attempts of institutions and official discourses to deny them. Both mock 'a distorted cartoon world... which would deny sexuality ·and physicality and insist on... reticence, a romantic view of love and an imposed orderliness. They oppose this world with the deliberate bad taste of rude words and farting elephants'.[1] The naughtiness of the films has long been obsolete in a more liberalised cinema, but the continuing prudishness of television validates the anachronistically transgressive pleasures which *That's Life* offers.

This anachronistic populism is complemented by the celebrated street interviews. They, too, display an obsessive level of sexual innuendo, implying that beneath the inhibited surface of the average British shopper lie hidden depths of carnival sexual energy. An energy which *That's Life* celebrates as the source of the 'innate genius of ordinary people'. 'Geniuses really do walk down every street. I've proved that.'[2] There are no stars on *That's Life* because we are all 'stars'. For what is continuously affirmed by the talking and performing pets, the small children with 'adult' talents, the musical performances without musical instruments, is that beneath the ossified layer of conventional social relations through which we daily experience an impersonal mass society is a potentially infinite fund of protean energy which only has to be released for a spontaneous blossoming of individual self-expression. And it is the business of *That's Life* to effect that release.

But it is also the business of *That's Life* to redress the wrongs done to the consumer. The consumer stories are generated by the breakdown of the 'natural' rituals of exchange and consumption in the social market-place (never production: redundancies? safety hazards? health risks? That's not Life). For in the sphere of exchange which Marx called 'an Eden of the innate rights of man' lurk serpents who violate the market's harmonious laws. The narratives of the programme dramatise their exposure and expulsion from the garden, restoring the prelapsarian harmony for another week.

The individuals in the stories – whether a suffering tenant, a frustrated consumer, a victim of professional malpractice – are only represented by still photographs which are either snapshots or use snapshot conventions. Rather than have the protagonists represent themselves (as in *Checkpoint* or *For What It's Worth*) *That's Life* dramatises their stories within the studio. The team act out the 'roles' involved as Rantzen relates the narrative. The ' innocent' viewers are cast as the perennial victims of greedy petit bourgeois capitalists, corrupt professionals, and faceless bureaucratic tyrants. Consequently the discourse of *That's Life* abstracts people's concrete experience of a social system *structurally* dependent upon the unequal distribution of resources into its own *individualised* demonology. We all become protagonists in an eternal mythological drama of struggle between 'us' and 'them' which can only be resolved by the *deus ex machina* of *That's Life* itself.

The essence of *That's Life*'s mythology is the denial of its own discourse and its insistence that the programme merely reproduces the 'real lives' of its audience. Every item, no matter how trivial, is introduced with a personalised acknowledgement of the viewer whose letter or phone-call initiated it. 'The (programme)... is really made by the public joining in and having a go... "The screen is two-way," says Esther.' As both source and destination of the programme 'we' become the producers of the *That's Life* mythology. Together 'we' see what 'Life' has thrown us this week, although only the team decide which bits of life are *That's Life*.

As Karl Marx once argued, within the social relations of capitalism we experience the external world as

'something alien and objective... confronting individuals not as their relation to one another, but as their subordination to relations which subsist independently of them... and which arise out of collisions between mutually indifferent individuals.'[3]

That's Life mythologises this generalised sense of alienation by creating a mythical dualism which opposes a rulebound/conventional/repressive/structural/official world with the energy of a libidinous/anarchic/communal/spontaneous/commonsensical populism.

Popular culture has always contained such a politically ambivalent opposition. It is continually shifting between a conservative fatalistic commonsense ('that's the way it is and always will be') and an immanent subversive energy which can invert the dominant symbolic order (the disruptions of theological orthodoxy in medieval carnival) and resist an oppressive system with the force of utopian desire (the circus in *Hard Times*). *That's Life* harnesses the themes and conventions of urban working-class culture to fuel its own mythology while suppressing its collective subversive energy. The 'Them' and 'Us' of a *class* popular culture become the 'Them' and 'Us' of a *consumer* popular culture. The bowlers of the imitation bosses people used to throw things at on Blackpool's pleasure beach are transmuted into the gold-peaked hats of *That's Life*'s 'Jobsworth' awards given to anyone who stands by a stupid rule because it's more than their 'jobsworth' to break it. (With four million unemployed not, perhaps, that unreasonable.) The popular forms used to express collective historical experience are appropriated to construct a mythology of individual 'consumers' outside history and outside class.

This mythology represents our historical experience of a specific system as the ahistorical experience of 'life'. Esther Rantzen: 'I sometimes think God writes the script. We simply take it over and reap the benefit.' But an effective mythology must seem to provide (mythical) solutions for our real (historical) problems. *That's Life*, as the embodiment of the populist will, prides itself on being a transformational programme achieving concrete resolutions for the difficulties of its viewers. But God is a singularly selective scriptwriter who ensures that only problems which are resolvable within the mythology are selected. Despite the global ambitions of its title, *That's Life*'s discourse can only incorporate individual anomalies in the sphere of exchange (which can be ameliorated through consumer regulations), isolated instances of deprivation with an obvious scapegoat, or a 'natural tragedy' which can be prevented by the 'goodheartedness of ordinary people'. When *That's Life* draws attention to an ill pensioner having to live in damp accommodation, it unhesitatingly points the finger of righteousness at the council responsible. The following week the council has been spurred into action and donations and offers of help from viewers have solved the problem. But the lowest level of housing investment since the 1920s is unmentioned, because to do so would pose problems which can only be resolved through the political and historical process which is invisible in *That's Life*'s mythological world.

Whatever their 'real' efficacy, *That's Life*'s interventions remain mythical because they operate in a 'magical' way which is outside the normal political processes, and indeed they are accorded the power of magic because of a generalised popular alienation from those processes, which are represented as part of the structured 'official' world which *That's Life* transcends. Not only is this congruent with the populist appeal of anti-statist Thatcherism to the 'peoples'' will, to the mythical 'Us', to turn against the 'Them' of the bureaucratic establishment, in the name of the sovereign freedom of the consumer. It also, by concentrating exclusively on the individualised sphere of consumption and exchange, confines the limits of possible change to the elimination of particular evils from the market. The system of production which actually generates them is represented as norma- tive, 'life' itself, and therefore beyond change. The significance of *That's Life*'s mythology is that it incorporates the potentially subversive energies of popular culture into what Barthes calls the inoculation effect which 'immunises the contents of the collective imagination by means of a small inoculation of acknowledged evil; one thus protects . . . against the risk of a generalised subversion'.[4]

The affairs of mice and men gang aft agley, and it's always tempting to shrug 'That's life!' *That's Life*'s own reduction of history into mythology reveals what is often at stake in that temptation – for the moment we say 'that's life' we have come out of the cold of the history which we make and into the warm fireside of myth which is made for us. For myth thrives in that space culture designates as outside history, the space that's life.

Notes

1. Marion Jordan. 'Carry On – Follow that Stereotype'. *British Cinema History*. Eds. James Curran. Vincent Porter. Weidenfield and Nicholson. 1983. p. 326.
2. *That's Life*. W. H. Allen. Esther Rantzen. p. 7.
3. K. Marx. *Grundrisse*. Penguin. 1973. p. 157.
4. R. Barthes. *Mythologies*. Granada. 1973. p. 150.

Philip Simpson

One Man and his Dog Show

Outside, the light fades behind a terrace of houses and a mild spring evening grows darker. Short-distance urban commuters are getting home by congested rail or road, crossing the border between two distinct lives: work and colleagues on one side, family and some leisure on the other. Going home in London, even the extent to which you can stretch your legs in the train, or on the streets, is circumscribed by the numbers of others all wanting to do the same. If you look out for it, you can tell the time of year by the tiny gardens or by the state of the trees planted a century ago to break up the monotony of the rows of houses. You can also tell by the noises: voices, laughter, reggae, rock, stand out against the whoosh-whoosh-whoosh and more generalised rumble of car and bus traffic.

A mild evening light brings on the street life and shows up the delapidation; it also brings out the stylish clothes of the punks in the pub garden at the street corner. The colour of the sky is a rough guide to the time of day, but there are few places in London where you can see the sun setting at the level of the horizon: normally you can see, between buildings either side of the street, about forty-five degrees of the sun's journey. Everything seems constricted and contrasted in a city, with what is fresh for a day at odds with what is decaying from the past, like the funk band poster stuck on the cast-iron lamp-post. Class contrasts are dramatised in the city by the down-and-outs shacked up in cardboard boxes by the station, and the groups stepping from taxis to the foyer of the opera house within a hundred yards.

One Man and his Dog offers to set so much of this to rights. In place of a sharp distinction between work and the rest of life, its images are of a life of work perfected into a satisfying craft and displayed as an exemplar. The work itself depends upon technology no higher than a whistle, and the programme carefully excludes any traces of the mechanical or electronic devices that are central to urban life. Even a Land Rover would seem anachronistic: the instant communication and rapid movement which characterise work in a city are replaced by shouts, whistles, and a man and dog running. Against the assault by the manufactured noises of work or play, which is constant in most lives, the sounds of the programme are beautifully definite and assertively 'natural': wind and water, abrupt commands, occasional thunder, all captured and relayed to us with a transparent simplicity and directness made possible by advanced technology and sophisticated production skills.

Against the limitations upon the space you can see (let alone use) in an urban setting, the locations of *One Man and his Dog* systematically offer vistas to a far horizon, suggesting freedom and possibilities open to the singular man and his servant. Actual sheep-dog trials are often carried out over terrain which can be rugged and dull, but here the shepherd is set against a landscape such that when his dogs run out to 'lift and fetch', in the active jargon of the programme, the camera can sweep in the classic elements of rural imagery – nearby fields, distant hills, a patterned sky and reflecting water. Where, when coming home from work we see the changes due to the time of day and year, here the camera seems to reveal nature as the fundamental source of these changes, when it lingers to give images of skyscapes well beyond the narrative needs of the programme. Unlike other televised sports, where matters of action and question carry forward the narrative, matters for contemplation find space in *One Man and his Dog*.

Hinting at space and freedom in its images of nature, the programme nevertheless insists, particularly in its commentary, upon the social values of discipline, control and practicality. But it turns these aspects of behaviour into elements of a rural ideal to put before urban viewers. Where urban life seems unbearably constricted and on the edge of chaos, or days at work slip by and you have the feeling that nothing has been done, *One Man and his Dog* suggests a kind of work where clear results of a practical kind are achievable through self-discipline and control by the shepherd and his dog. Dislocation is, of course, always present as a possibility: threatening weather is noted, an over-excited dog reprimanded by commentator Eric Halsall, and the sheep did turn very nasty on Anne McCullough and Shep in the Junior Championship. But the exercise of control and discipline to practical ends restores order, and receives praise and points from the commentator and the judges. Endurance of hardship by man and dog, and their mutual submission to a tough regimen are features of rural life of which we are reminded by Phil Drabble, whose role it is to call the audience to the programme; but the unstated message is one of an environment brought under control. It is also an image of control that seems to owe nothing to economic or juridical laws, but depends upon a personal relationship between a man and a subordinated creature. The harmony and practicality of that relationship contrasts with its urban parallel where a notice on every other lamp-post in my street officially connotes 'dogs' with 'nuisance'.

Harmony is carefully maintained even in the potentially dangerous terrain of national competition. Over the eight programmes which make a series, shepherds from the four countries of the United Kingdom compete to become British champion, and each pair of competitors is introduced in a short film with a commentary by Phil Drabble. The films show each shepherd's home background but, though the commentary notes the differences in kind of farm or geographical location, the images speak of common experience – hard work, family life, moderate means. The pattern of each brief pictorial essay is similar, and the programme as a whole has formal camera routines which treat each competitor the same. The predictable close-ups of the men show faces which seem to have weathered sunlight, rain and wind impassively. All look well, but without the super-fit, high gloss of the spruce stars of track and field sports who appear in the *Grandstand* studio. It is the appearance of 'the natural' that is signalled in these faces and bodies to set against both those in the street and those of other sportsmen enhanced by steroids or emaciated by masochistic training routines.

Their clothing also has its meaning. It looks like a better cared-for version of what we see them wearing in the short biopics, and tones well with the setting, in the manner of the British 'country clothing' convention. Nothing looks sponsored or fashionable; the jackets, trousers and caps only grudgingly follow changes in styles since the war. Younger shepherds sometimes wear light-weight, shower-resistant anoraks, but personal styling like Navratilova's or Coe's is absent, and the commercialised national colours worn by the home countries' football teams would seem absurd. So, because the men look so much alike and are presented in activities which emphasise social and class similarities, the differences suggested by national origin are both offered and contained.

Most striking to the urban viewer, though, is the absence of black or brown faces. Black sportsmen are now a familiar sight on British television, but *One Man and his Dog* is one of the sports, like golf or horse-racing, where the multi-ethnic composition of British society is not reflected. Through making a television sport out of a pre-industrial craft, *One Man and his Dog* secures a sporting enclave into which the political and racial tensions which much sport now dramatises cannot intrude.

The conflicts in styles of living and social values now inescapable in any multi-ethnic metropolis cannot find a place in a programme that offers but a muted echo of differences between Anglo-Saxon, Celt and Gael. At their most pronounced, these differences are present in the accents of the participants when they talk about the work and leisure skills which they have in common. The programme itself manages the differences and competitiveness that might divide audiences with all the skill of the good shepherd and his dogs; it displays well television's propensity to lift, fetch, drive, pen and (occasionally) shed viewers like sheep. Eric and Phil do the kind of 'sophisticated brace-work' they admire in the dogs. Whenever I've seen it, though, the sheep have always been white.

But we television viewers are not sheep, and exercise choices without caring too much about shepherding by scheduling. As many viewers as watch Channel 4's most popular programmes watch *One Man and his Dog*, and the last series competed with a range of plays and films on ITV and Channel 4. We watch it, I think, because it offers an enclave of possibilities not often present in our lives, particularly those of us living in large cities. The possibilities it offers, though, are of yesterday's world: television's technological resources are deployed to construct a pre-urban ideal where life is unified and whole, where man and nature are in organic relationship, and where social divisions are less acute than shared experiences. It's a life in which we see men and women at work, and where the woman's subordination is plain even when it is clear that she is a domestic worker *and* a farm worker. (It must be said, though, that women shepherds do take part and are *not* called shepherdesses.) Children don't always follow their father's career: the Young Shepherd's competition had finalists who worked in offices and in the building trade, but the family is imaged so often as the unit supporting the father.

Parallels with rustic feudal idylls might be too neat. As I've already said, Phil Drabble emphasises the hardness of the shepherd's life, and the occasional items on country pursuits do hint at the way sheep breeding, for instance, has been altered by market forces. Nor is there a Lord of the Manor or church as any obvious voice of power or authority, and both Eric Halsall and Phil Drabble have a populist role. But the backward-looking and, I suppose, reactionary character of the programme is indicated in the way judgements are made and never questioned. In our world, High Court judges and tennis umpires are more visible and more challenged than ever, but the judges and the Course Director of *One Man and his Dog* are rarely glimpsed, and their decisions are never questioned. One way of preventing clashes with authority is for authority to remain hidden.

For me, *One Man and His Dog* is not a sinister or dangerous programme, though I can understand the arguments that would see it as such. Aware of its pleasure, and unable to feel a Barthesian sense of outrage at another victory for conformist realism, I have tried to sort out the satisfactions it seems to offer. Like most viewers, I watch it with a relaxed attention, often doing other things meanwhile, and only gradually does the kind of escape it offers become clear. A little more reflection alerts me to the skill with which the series is made. What seems an easy access to a world of order, space and unity is, of course, the effect of a process of production which elaborately effaces itself as a process. Where *are* the cameras and sound equipment whose records are cut together to make such a seamless whole? How much material is left out? Does the dubbed-on commentary *deliberately* attempt to give the impression that the outcome of the competition is still to be settled? How do we manage to pick up the technical terms and the criteria for assessment without paying real attention? How can such a didactic programme be so entertaining?

Simply knowing that *One Man and his Dog* is, in the last analysis, a programme using all the deceptive apparatus of realism to create a world free of problems, doesn't destroy or exhaust my pleasure in that world. And my pleasure doesn't blind me to the contrast with the outside world or incapacitate me from acting in it. *One Man and his Dog* offers a world in which I would not *want* to live: the disorder, contrasts, conflicts and struggles of the everyday world are preferable to the suppressions, repressions, feigned innocence and implied values of that fictive world. It's just too simple to be much help – or harm. Conscious of the programme's social regressiveness and distance from urban life, then, I conclude the programme meets a need I share with three or four million others.

Circuses met that need for the urban proletariat of 19th century England, according to Dickens, and were defended by him through the circus master, Sleary, who said in *Hard Times*:

'People must be amused. They can't be always a learning, nor yet they can't be always a working, they an't made for it. You must have us, Squire. Do the wise thing and the kind thing too, and make the best of us, not the worst.'

Television entertainment does meet some needs. Making the best of it, not the worst, probably is the kindest thing, and it may even be the wisest thing just now.

Rosalind Brunt

What's My Line?

It is 1984 in Britain and unemployment has officially reached $3\frac{1}{2}$ million and between 4 – 5 million unofficially. In March, the country's miners start a bitter and protracted struggle for the right to work. In the same month, television revives its most popular programme about the world of work, asking one basic question: 'And what do you do for a living?'

What's My Line?[1] was last broadcast nationwide from 1951–'63 on BBC. The period exactly coincided with an unbroken run of Conservative administrations, now recalled as The Age of Affluence and characterised as an era of relatively full employment and a boom time for consumer goods, such as television sets. For those who experienced the fifties, *What's My Line?* is remembered as the most popular game show of the period, associated with the novelty of early television viewing, the BBC in its 'Aunty' phase and families together as Sunday evening audiences. It evokes that cosy and comparatively secure interval between post-war austerity and the breakup of moral and political consensus signalled by 'permissiveness' in the sixties and reinforced later by economic slump.

Like all games shows, *What's My Line?* is crucial to audience 'ratings' strategy, particularly in a period of recession, when broadcasting companies play safe and go for successful formulas they can recycle. The management decision to revive the show in the eighties recognised the audience appeal of a 'return to the fifties' with a specific scheduling operation to create a 'nostalgia package'. Transferred to ITV, the show became the early evening 'hook' on Monday nights at 7.00, creating an 'inheritance factor' which, in schedulers' parlance, 'delivered the audience' for *Coronation Street* at 7.30. As many have pointed out, *Coronation Street*, though based on contemporary working-class life in Lancashire, actually harks back to a utopian version of a fifties 'organic community'. Pushed together, the two programmes offer an hour of time securely frozen in the fifties – apart from the discontinuities of the advertising breaks – with old-fashioned production values, naturalistic and unobtrusive, to match.

What's My Line? offers further guarantees of stability and continuity with the fifties by preserving its original format in minutest detail. It was the show which first created the British 'TV personality' according to certain character-types. And here they are again: the male comic turn, the vamp, the older, 'wise woman' (originally Lady Isobel Barnett), the crusty gentleman (most famously, Gilbert Harding). Two of the original personalities have returned: the Canadian actress, Barbara Kelly (as the vamp turned wise woman) and Eamonn Andrews, the presenter, who first set the broadcasting mould of 'genial and charming Irishman' subsequently adopted by Terry Wogan in the BBC game show, *Blankety Blank*.

The format is straightforward and easy to follow. The object of the game is that a panel of five celebrities (enlarged to include the category 'sophisticated, handsome man' positioned between the two women panellists) guess what a series of 'challengers' do 'for a living'. After 10 wrong guesses, the challenger receives a scroll for 'beating the panel'. Half-way through 'it's time for the blindfolds' and a Mystery Guest is introduced who puts on a disguised voice. The programme is punctuated by a series of familiar rituals: the presenter introduces the panel: each challenger is asked to 'sign in please' (with a signature written large) and this is followed by 'a piece of mime, please' (about the job) and a caption description viewers can shut their eyes for. The presenter both adjudicates and helps the challenger sitting beside him to answer the panel's questions. Questioning is based on particular definitions of work and aimed at avoiding a 'no' answer with jokey double negatives and convolutions like: 'Would I be right in thinking that you are *not* a...?' After each game, challengers are often prompted to relate a brief anecdote about their work. The Mystery Guest in the middle gets a longer chat, and shakes hands with the panel. And the show closes with the presenter signing everybody off till next week.

There are two main formulae for television game shows. The first is based on a host (with 'hostesses') adjudicating between members of the public who compete for prizes. The second, the panel game, relies much less on audience participation and the associated razzamatazz of competitive suspense. Rather, it sustains audience interest through the quality of its interactions between personalities and public. As a panel game, *What's My Line?* relies on the audience's understanding that they are watching not a competition but *an entertainment*.

The show is 'entertaining' in two related senses. It is both 'hospitable' and 'amusing'. The presenter must observe host-guest courtesies of welcoming introductions and conversational induce-ments, as in a chat show, whilst also referring to the conventions of showbiz humour and eliciting 'performances' from all the parti-cipants which are directed outwards to both studio and home audiences. The laughter and applause of the unseen studio audience is an essential programme ingredient for underscoring the presenter's courtesies and showing appreciation of all performances. It also gives 'clues' to inform the panel's guessing game. But since the competitive element is reduced to a jokey formality between presenter and panel, the audience's main function is to respond to the programme's humour, to indicate, albeit invisibly, that they are thoroughly 'at home' with the entertainment.

The humour of the programme works chiefly by insinuation and *double entendre*. It is based on the implication that all jobs are potentially funny. Since the audience is already in the know about each contestant's job, the unknowing panel keeps up humour with 'knowing' questions. The staple joke of the programme is: 'do you provide a *service*?' with developments like: 'and could I *avail* myself of this service?/would you come to my *home* to do this?/is what you do *naughty*?/could you do it to *me*?' (producing gales of studio laughter when addressed to a turkey stuffer, for instance).

The 'service' routine is often combined with a view of the human body as intrinsically hilarious. For instance, in this exchange between a plump panellist, George Gale (the Gilbert Harding figure), and an (unknown to him, yet) corsetière:

GG: You must be producing some service for the rest of us – is that right?

Challenger: Yes, a certain amount of people who need it.

GG: And am I right in thinking I *might* need it? (studio laughter now punctuates the whole exchange).

C: You could do, Mr. Gale!

GG: Would I prefer *not* to need it?

C: Er, yes.

Eamonn Andrews: Yes, er –

GG: Hang on, that's a 'yes'.

EA: I think I'd be helping you to give you a 'no', but *I'll* have it.

GG: Would you – er, do this in *my* house?

C: Oh, no!

E.A.: – Yes, um, I won't say any more, it would only lead you astray!...

Barbara Kelly: Is beauty and shape of *flesh* anything to do with it? Do you work below the neck – if you'll pardon the expression? (applause)...

E.A.: She's beaten the panel! I adjudicate! She's a 'corsetière' – is that how you pronounce it? (panel and audience laughter). Can you imagine George going round in a corset!? There you are, and I've no time to tell you about her Royal Warrant (music faded up). It's goodnight from Eric Morecambe, Jilly Cooper, Jeffrey Archer, Barbara Kelly and the uncorsetted George Gale. Until next week – goodbye. (9.4.84).

The jokes are only slightly risqué. They remain within the boundaries of urbane politeness and are never blue and loud. But the show takes for granted that women, by their very nature, are an automatic source of humour. The show adopts a routine tone of genteel sexism towards women which is intended to be inoffensive because offered as a courtesy-ritual. However, its effect is a continual bantering discomfiture of women challengers. In the same show, the first challenger is rendered giggly and inarticulate both by the comic 'service' routine and by repeated, flattering references to her attractiveness: 'and a *very* beautiful first challenger it is too . . . *such* a pretty lady . . . are you the prettiest traffic warden in London?' And the next challenger, a male saddler, is asked in the anecdote spot:

E.A.: And why were you involved in making a saddle for Zsa Zsa Gabor? (studio titter).

C: Why?!!! (howls of laughter).

Eric Morecambe: I'd leave it at that if I were you!

E.A.: (smiling) Right, rather leave it at that, thank you. Thank you, Eric, you've probably fallen off the same saddle yourself, is that it?

There is an approximate balance of men and women challengers on the show. Of the six programmes I watched in the 15-week series, this is what their captions said:

Women: traffic warden, corsetière, bus driver, belt-and-braces maker, ERNIE operator, Easter egg maker, turkey stuffer, crab fisher, sleeping bag stuffer, 'She makes Boy George's collar jackets', pyjama corder, flower seller.

Men: saddler, Forth Rail Bridge painter, Morris dancer, sporran maker, butterfly farmer, pheasant plucker, bosun's mate, bottle washer, fish cake maker, billiard table leveller, sundial designer.

The style of job has not changed since the fifties. On the first *What's My Line?* of 1951 the jobs were: street trader, chauffeuse, cocktail shaker and swimming instructress. All the jobs are intended to be recognised by the audience as odd or peculiar in some way – and when the captions go up there is always laughter with the applause. The choice of some of the women's jobs is intended to 'surprise' traditional gender roles, but the show always returns gender to its proper place: the requirements of courtesy insist that the challenger is, of course, much too feminine to be undertaking such a tough job. The men's jobs rarely step out of gender role and usually involve higher status and earning power.

What both men's and women's jobs have in common is that they are humorous because incongruous: somehow quirky, eccentric, unlikely. But their very atypicality is precisely what makes them 'typical'. They are 'peculiarly British' jobs. The show appeals to commonsense myths of a British national identity composed of ordinary people who are in fact all 'originals', unique and individualistic, with certain 'peculiarities'. The choice of challengers on *What's My Line?* appeals to a Britishness which 'all of us' are assumed to share: an enjoyment of eccentricity and an ability to laugh at ourselves – as transmitted and endorsed by one of Britain's favourite Irishmen.

The appeal to the typically British contains the show's promise to transcend the class barriers that get in the way of everyday life. But *What's My Line?* is actually quite class-specific. The dominant work-ethos associated with all the challengers' jobs is a petit bourgeois and entrepreneurial one, with an emphasis on people working for themselves, and on their own, in small businesses with a traditional craft background. The show's ethos is reinforced by the challengers' appearances as individuals in their own right. And the type of anecdote they tell about their 'line' is about special awards, meetings with royalty, a humorous occasion. All of which suggests the idea of work as an *amateur* notion, a fascinating hobby for which payment is incidental.

Yet it is clear, even from my small sample, that a number of the jobs, especially the women's, are not of this character at all, but low-paid, casual or unskilled working-class jobs, often performed collectively and in bad environments. But reference to real-life conditions is ruled out by the entertainment context of the show. Politeness and humour inhibit direct mention of class – and class distinctions are blurred by the way each challenger's job is set up in the introduction. Four 'clues' are given: first, the signing-in ceremony, which proclaims the challenger as a unique individual; the disembodied mime, implying an absence of social and productive relations; then the request 'tell the panel which part of Britain you are from', informing us that regionality is more significant than class anyway. Finally, Eamonn Andrews states how each challenger is paid. According to the show's three categories, the terms are: 'salaried', 'self-employed', or 'fee-earning' (as with the Morris dancer). The polite device of 'salaried' to cover both monthly earnings and weekly or hourly waged work eludes the real class distinctions between jobs. All jobs are rendered classless when Eamonn Andrews declares that each one is middle-class.

By combining the double entertainment strategies of hospitality and amusement, *What's My Line?* effectively absorbs the class realities of each challenger's job and buries them in a nationally-unified context of genial Britishness. As for the panel and Mystery Guests, because they constitute the main entertainment function of the programme, it is not obvious that their performances relate directly to their own 'lines' of work. But their reason for being on the show is, importantly, to ensure continuity of employment in the celebrity world of media/showbiz/bestsellerdom to which they all belong. For they are mainly individual freelancers who must depend on a constant supply of public appearances for successive work contracts. And to work as a gameshow panellist is to enhance personality, status and hence the fee that can be commanded. To appear on *What's My Line?*, therefore, requires little individual adjustment to its prevailing entrepreneurial ethos.

But Eamonn Andrews doesn't introduce the panel by saying they are in the studio to make a living. Instead he says (fade up music):

'Hello there and welcome. And do you know I've just realised that we're very upmarket this week that, er, we have *three* novelists in a row on our panel here. Taking time off from his *fourth* novel, although you know him slightly better as a comedian – Eric Morecambe (applause; E.M.: Good evening, I thank you, thanks). Er, as well as being a novelist, our next panellist is of course a *journalist* and she's written factual books as well, such as, you know, *The British in Love* and *Class* – of which she has more than her fair share – Jilly Cooper (applause; J.C. laughs). And a former Member of Parliament who is now an international bestseller with such novels you know so well as *Cain and Abel*, *A Quiverful of Arrows* – and he hopes to be on target tonight – Jeffrey Archer (applause). And Barbara Kelly, who's so good at this game now that Bernie Braden tells me it's quite normal in the morning for her to say 'I'm not wrong, am I, in saying that you'd like two boiled eggs for breakfast?' (laughter, applause). Former editor of the *Spectator* and *Express* columnist, who, they tell me, his bite is worse than his bark – George Gale. Right, you know the rules by now. So will our first challenger *sign in* please! (9.4.84).

Other media sources of information reveal the real economic circumstances of the panel. For instance, Jilly Cooper has described in her newspaper columns how the two books referred to in her introduction were written as a direct and hasty consequence of her husband's bankruptcy. And it is public record that Jeffrey Archer turned to bestsellerdom following a crashed speculative venture that forced his resignation as a Conservative M.P. Such examples only highlight the extent to which the world of economic determination does not impinge on the amusing context of *What's My Line?*

The final ingredient of the show, the Mystery Guest's appearance, does nothing to make the programme more directly related to the context of real life – although he or she is usually chosen for topicality. Since the show is always 'live from London' their reasons for being there are usually connected with some commodity for sale. They have just written a book, for instance (Barbara Cartland), are opening in a show (Petula Clarke) or have won an award (Bob Champion). But as they cannot directly advertise, the entrepreneurial nature of their appearances must be again disguised beneath the programme's repartee and banter. Thus in the programme already quoted, the Mystery Guest, a photographer, is first asked by the presenter after his identity is revealed: You've written a book about it (photography), haven't you?

Mystery Guest: Yeah – but I've also taken a picture of Jeffrey for the back of his er -- is it out yet, Jeffrey?

Jeffrey Archer: No, not till July, Denis.

M.G.: I don't want to advertise – I'm trying to advertise *me* rather than you, actually! (laughter).

J.A.: I do, though! (laughter).

The Mystery Guest is Denis Healey and Eamonn Andrews goes on to ask him how he started. He says ' . . . I was *lucky.* I went abroad a great deal and so I had some interesting pictures to show.' It is routine procedure on panel and chat shows for guests to consign the successes of their lives to the contingent and tactful realm of 'luck'. On this occasion, emphasis on the 'luck' of Denis Healey in his role as celebrity photographer and TV personality encourages the audience to forget that they are watching the self-same person who, as Labour Chancellor of the Exchequer in the mid-seventies, started implementing the sort of public spending cuts and redefining the government's 'social contract' with the working class in a way which prepared the ground for the contemporary Conservative strategy of mass unemployment.

This is how the programme copes with that 'other' Healey:

Eamonn Andrews: You have a reputation for being a very serious politician, of course, but also of being a bit of a joker – er – would you have gone into – er – listening to that accent (the disguised voice) – theatre or showbusiness, had you not gone into the other –

Denis Healey: When I was at school I acted *brilliantly* (laughter). My first part was Polly Perkins in the *Great Cham's Diamond*. Did you ever read that? (further anecdotes about acting)... I was quite keen on it – but you know, if you're a politician, you don't need to go on the stage really! (laughter).

E.A.: Denis Healey – a pleasure having you with us and thank you very much.

In the world of *What's My Line?* all politicians are hams at heart and the political sphere is a passing show with no power to affect our daily lives. Outside the studio, there may be bankruptcies, wage cuts and job losses. But inside, thank goodness, we've still got a sense of humour. Being able to see the funny side of things, the audience watches the realities of 'making a living' transformed into an entertaining spectacle. In its fifties limbo, depoliticised and de-contextualised, *What's My Line?* is recycled for timeless repetition. When the programme comes off the air in early July, all over real Britain the miners' strike is entering its seventeenth week.

Notes

1.   For all its naturalised Britishness, *What's My Line?* originates from the USA. It was bought by the BBC in 1951 for 25 guineas a show from the American impresario, Maurice Winnick, the main promoter of the post-war panel game. The show's formula was devised by Mark Goodson and Bill Todman, ex-journalists who also created *The Name's the Same* (ITV) and *Twenty Questions* (BBC radio) of the same era.

Cary Bazalgette

All in Fun: Su Pollard on Disney Time

When holiday time comes round, you can always rely on television to join in the fun. If there isn't any fun, it can even provide some. On Bank Holiday Mondays, those special days when the 'average family' has nothing in particular arranged – some sport for Dad, maybe, or an outing for Mum and the kids, but no Christmas dinner, no Easter Eggs, no predictable rituals – then for this average family to which television, as we know, speaks with the most confidence, there can be something special after all, a bit out of the ordinary: a film that we'll all enjoy, a show with stars that we love, something that will confirm and validate our own pleasures.

Disney Time is a Bank Holiday winner, a tried and trusted formula now 25 years old. It's a simple formula, too. A currently popular TV star introduces a series of short extracts from Disney films. Scheduled around 5.00 p.m. on Bank Holidays and Christmas Day each year, it's an ideal way to occupy the kids for forty-five minutes while Mum makes the tea (though it's meant to be viewing for all the family). What makes it so innocuous, so innocently pleasurable?

In many ways, we know what to expect from a programme like this. We know, for instance, what 'family entertainment' is. It takes the place of children's TV at weekends and holiday time. Whereas children's TV is sharply marked off from the rest of TV with its own trailers and continuity presentation, family entertainment eases the national living room into its evening viewing. Early in the evening, when very young children are assumed to be watching, programmes address us all as children, both real children and the imagined, nostalgic child in every adult. We are reminded what childhood is supposed to be: powerless, vulnerable, but carefree and happy. We are given what children are expected to like: daft jokes, spectacular action, fantasy, magic and, above all, animals. In *this* space we can enjoy them, participate in the entertainment of our children. We expect frequent changes of scene or subject, and a certain kind of address to camera: gentle, patient, intimate, concerned, full of expression, usually smiling, often wide-eyed. An ideal relationship is offered to children, an ideal role to adults.

And then, *Disney Time* is about films. Like a post-revolutionary state, maintaining the palaces of former oppressors in order to instruct and amaze the proletariat, television keeps on teaching us about cinema. Films are shown, stars interviewed, compilations assembled, genres parodied. Critics speak and buffs compete. Most of us may never set foot in a cinema, but television knows that we can all still recognize the nostalgic iconography of cinema: floodlit block-piled letters, folding canvas chairs with names on the back, Wurlitzers, and satin flounced curtains. The mime of cranking a silent film camera can be understood even by children born 50 years after the advent of sound. Programmes actually *about* cinema usually offer us a particular way of looking at and understanding it – one that reminds us of, and confirms, everyday talk about films, that is, re-telling each other the good bits. It's rare for a programme to concentrate, as *Disney Time* does, on the work of one director and studio. This can only be done, of course, when, as in the case of Disney, the product is pre-sold, and is more than just films. Fifty years of merchandizing have established the Disney characters – usually defined as the *lovable* Disney characters – as household figures. *Disney Time* reminds us that 'Disney' is not just an animation director, but a studio with a range of products to sell: crazy comedies, for instance, or child-and-animal dramas; a studio with a carefully stage-managed re-releasing policy whereby its classics reappear on a seven-year cycle. Television is an essential part of this apparatus. Programmes such as *Disney Time* and *Mickey and Donald* keep the great name in our minds and whet our appetites for taking yet another generation of children to see that wonderful moment when...

Nostalgia is a mutually pleasurable way for adults to exercise power over children. It makes the past seem innocuous and enticing, and it teaches the importance of the unattainable, the things that happened, were seen, 'before you were born'. Through the nostalgic mode children are encouraged to acquire a similar stock of knowledge and source of story-telling. *Disney Time* follows this pattern. Nostalgic recollections of this song, that thrill, those side-splitting scenes, are interspersed with newer material, up-to-date releases. Disney's products offer a nostalgic process that you can buy into, acquire your own stock of 'wonderful moments when...'

Family entertainment, cinema, Disney – so far the predictable. The unpredictable element of the programme is the star. Unpre-dictable, because this is the star outside of the usual context. The attraction of the programme, for many perhaps the main attraction, is the chance to see the star outside the variety shows or sitcom from which we know them. This is a common device and an essential part of the way television stars are created. The programmes that import the stars can boost their ratings through the stars' attraction, but the stars also get the opportunity to extend their image and make it more complex.

Stardom has always set up processes of identification and the desire to know more and more about the star's 'real personality' and private life. But in televisual forms such as the sitcom or continuing serial, where the star constantly reappears in the *same* role rather than, as in the cinema, a series of possibly similar but nonetheless distinct roles, a particularly intimate relationship between star and audience is set up. Popular characters in these forms develop their own biographies. Regular viewers are rewarded for their loyalty by the special pleasures of recognizing the quirks of behaviour, subtle reactions and idiosyncrasies of their favourite performers – details that more fickle viewers might miss. The curiosity that will naturally arise when the opportunity is presented of seeing a star outside their usual, rigorously defined, context, is spiced with a little anxiety about how they will appear in this new situation. Just how different will they be? Will they manage the new role as well as they do the other one? Will the illusion be spoiled, or enhanced?

Whereas stars often appear 'in character' on other shows, the *Disney Time* tradition is to show them as 'themselves'. The formula thus becomes a little curious, setting up an elaborate tissue of meaning. The star is magically 'discovered' at home or at the seaside, or perhaps in a Christmas grotto, and speaks directly to us without the intervention of presenter or narrator. We are invited to share in reminiscence and pleasure about fragments of film which come, as it were, from nowhere and fill the screen. It's as though the star, on holiday like us, slips into *our* living rooms to watch the clips with us. Then there is the trail of memories and expectations that is drawn along with the star from their regular show. This is blended with what appear to be their choices, their own personal memories, of Disney classics. Some may actually be their favourites, and some of the presentation may be 'ad libbed' ; most clips are, however, chosen for them by the producer, Richard Evans, who also scripts their 'in character' linking patter. So how can this be unpredictable?

It's time to consider an actual *Disney Time*, an actual star in context. For the 1984 Spring Bank Holiday show, Su Pollard was chosen as presenter. Her major claim to fame was as Peggy Ollerenshaw, the 'potty chalet maid' in the Perry and Croft sitcom *Hi De Hi*, then already past its fourth series. Virtually unknown at first, Pollard was only one of the comedy ensemble representing staff at 'Maplin's Holiday Camp' in 1959, but her particular earnest, frizzy-haired, bespectacled variant on the dumb blonde stereotype proved vastly popular. Apart from appearing in children's shows and on commercials, by the summer of 1984 she was famous enough to feature in a Heineken poster which assumed general public awareness of Peggy's ambition to be transformed from a lowly chalet maid to a Maplin's Yellowcoat.

But on *Disney Time*, of course, Pollard appears not as Peggy but as 'herself'. What does this mean? Predominantly, it's a 'making strange' of the Peggy character without abandoning it altogether. Many of the Pollard/Peggy characteristics that we expect still appear. There is the sudden huddle forward of the body and sideways swivelling of the eyes as a confidence is uttered. There are the odd little sounds, a sort of 'hmmm!' halfway between a thoughtful murmur and a suppressed giggle, that punctuate every sentence, and the wide-eyed, wide-mouthed '*Anyway* . .' that signals the end of each digression. It's not exactly like Peggy, even if it reminds us of her. But in this context we recognize more – or at least some of us do. We recognize the body language and intonation of gossip – specifically, girls' gossip. Rather than the propriety of the older sister or nice auntie that children's presenters usually display, what we get here is something complicit with its audience – or half of it. It's the language of hiding behind the bike sheds or in the toilets, furtive and giggling, sisterly and anarchic.

For another characteristic that Pollard brings from Peggy and, indeed, from all the other dumb blondes in that long-lived tradition, is a potential for disruption. The dumb blonde has to be both more gullible, and more honest, than all the other characters – though she doesn't completely steal the show, of course, being contained, limited, by her sexuality. It's a bit different in Peggy's case: short-sighted, round-shouldered, all long nose and broad Northern accent, *she*'s contained by her comedy, by the incongruity of her desires. Pollard carries with her from Peggy the apparent safeness of comedy: all light-hearted fun and a bit daft, really. But as Pollard, alone and speaking directly to us, a different kind of incongruity emerges.

Surrounded by stuffed toys in a stark white room, wearing lace mittens, swansdown bracelets, red stockings and a frock patterned with Disney characters ('made it meself this morning'), she peers through big, red-tinted glasses, reciting her script obediently and tapping out the rhythm of the words on her knee: ' . . . and they're both chasing after this little caterpillar.' There's a pause. The eyes glaze, re-focus, apparently on us. ' . . . Or was it a worm? Oh, I dunno what they're trying to catch, do you?' – this last addressed to the giant stuffed dog on her lap. The zany persona, the kitsch clothes and decor, the 'let's all be naughty girls' intonation of the ad libs, all make a space, allow things to be said that can't often be said in popular entertainment.

Between another pair of clips, Pollard is discovered at the sink, languidly scrubbing pots. A red saucepan is inverted on her head and remains there, unremarked, throughout the scene. 'I'm fed up of this,' snaps Pollard in mid-script, ' – it's man's work.' Throwing the pot back in the sink, she comes to sit with us, as it were, at the kitchen table. 'I do *hate* housework,' she confides, just in case we thought she was like poor oppressed Peggy, polishing plugholes and ironing ten-shilling notes. Later, she introduces a set of Disney dolls. 'Now Minnie and I,' she announces, 'are going to watch the men create havoc in *Mickey's Fire Brigade*.' Then comes the muttered ad lib: 'Come on, Minnie, I bet the men mess it all up. You know what men are like, flippin' useless . . .'

What should we make of all this? It could be just part of that working-class female plaint, 'Tch – *men*!' – regular as clockwork in, say, *Coronation Street*. But Pollard is presented alone: 'Welcome to my new house! I'm still trying to get it organized – it takes ages' and every scene is lavishly filled with her possessions and decor. Is she an independent woman, then, setting up house alone and sniping at the men she's failed to get, or keep? Well, perhaps, but then *that's* contradicted by the stuffed toys, the girlish confidences, the signoff 'I have to go now because my dolls are starving – they go mad if I don't feed 'em.' Can Pollard possibly be trying to subvert our lovable Disney world, sneak a bit of feminist consciousness-raising into our family Bank Holiday viewing? Of course not: after all, it's just comedy, she's only Peggy, and it's all in fun. We don't expect serious ideas in family entertainment, the argument goes: *Threads* or the *Man Alive Debate* might change people's lives but *Disney Time* isn't likely to.

It's odd, in fact, how critics from both Right and Left concur in identifying what's politically significant on TV, where its potential for signalling or expressing change may lie. Popular forms are castigated for their conformity and innocuousness, but it could be that their very safety makes a space for changes of a different kind. Rather than the subversive *content* that draws such attention to itself, Pollard offers us the possibility of subversive *readings*. Mickey's fire brigade, for instance, becomes not so much a bevy of winsome eccentrics as a bunch of incompetents who meet their deserved comeuppance when they tangle with the mighty Claribel Cow. It's still funny, but probably not quite what Disney had in mind.

I should like to thank Richard Evans, the producer of *Disney Time*, for the help he has given me.

Bob Ferguson

Black Blue Peter

On 24 June, 1984, *Blue Peter* was presented by pretty green-eyed Janet Ellis, farmer's son Simon Groom and a man called Peter Duncan. (The biographical details can be found in the BBC/Scholastic Publications *Blue Peter* book published in 1983.) The programme contained the following items in chronological order:
1. A Song of Praise from the Angelical Voice Choir.
2. A short piece on two young skaters: Paul Knepper and Natasha Smith.
3. Three recipes presented by Peter Duncan and Janet Ellis.
4. A story about Prince Lee Boo.
5. Two more songs from the Angelical Voice Choir.

It is the intention of this short piece to examine the various discourses, explicit and implicit, to be found in a single edition of a programme now in its 26th year. It is a programme which epitomises the naturalisation processes by which ideology is purveyed and cumulative myths find their material forms. I shall concentrate on the 'multi-cultural' elements in the programme, though it will be necessary to show how these are interwoven with the more usual stories in a process of ideological work designed to unite, at the very least, *Blue Peter* viewers in a world at once homogenised and free from contradiction.

The Angelical Voice Choir is made up of young black Christians who had been singing together for only three months by the middle of June, 1984.

'As little as that!' says Simon to their conductor later in the show. 'Well, you've achieved a tremendous amount in a short space of time. Well done!'

Blue Peter is a programme that specialises in saying 'well done' to its viewers, the participants and, ultimately, to itself. *Blue Peter* has, in one quarter of a century, become the BBC's mouthpiece for all that is youthful, pure and good. It has been able to unite a nebulous group of parents[1] and children around televisual discourses which allow for charity, caring, the removal of history and the denial of struggle for change. It is a perverse ideologue's dream.

The first shots of the programme in question show the Angelical

Voice Choir in action. They are nervous, vibrant, enthusiastic. That enthusiasm is taken up by the near cheer which they elicit from the three presenters who are seated on a sofa watching them, with us, of course. The choir is congratulated for getting the show off to 'an electrifying start.' The ability of black choirs to electrify the white presenters with their rhythm is a theme to which they, and we the viewers, will return.

We move on to the short feature on the young skaters who are linked, having once skated in the same programme, with the names of two others dearly beloved of *Blue Peter* – Torville and Dean. The young skaters work hard and train regularly and their dedication is lauded. Their trainer, it is pointed out, will settle for nothing less than perfection. They discuss their unified ambition to make it to the top and eventually to train others. They are the potential participants in a fairy tale yet to be constructed.

But the real centre of this little feature is Janet Ellis. She presents the whole piece in a style reminiscent of the schoolgirl heroines to be found in Hutchinson's Girls' Annuals of the 1940s:

'As I took my first faltering steps on the ice, I was relieved the others were too busy to notice me.'

It is an essentially middle-class discourse which, in intonation and structure, has a flirtatious yet vaguely patronising quality. Janet recognises young talent on our behalf, whilst endearing herself to us by her engaging failure as a skater. She is a contradictory figure, friendly, yet distanced by her Christopher Robin voice; cheekily chaste.

The training session is followed by a brief performance by the young skaters in the empty ice rink. They dance their routine to the tune of 'In the Mood', a well-known Glen Miller number and the signature tune of the Joe Loss Orchestra. We then return to the studio where Simon makes a brief quip about the skating having got us all in the mood. This humorous badinage is presumably intended for parents, for it is hardly likely that many child viewers will know the title of the piece. It is a little joke for those of us who are in the know. It is also another element which recurs in the discourses of children's television – that of providing the means for patting oneself on the back whilst being blinded to the naturalisation process to which one is being subjected. It is another of those inconsequential and yet crucial moments when an unspoken 'well-done' is being bestowed upon those eligible to receive it.

And so we move, with the easy flow so characteristic of a world beyond contradiction, into the presentation and demonstration of three recipes by "Chef Duncan." We are told it is barbecue time now that summer is here and the implication is that all (normal) people will, of course, have their own barbecue in the garden. If you live in a tower block in Rotherhithe, such as many of the people featured by their absence in the story which follows, presumably you would go to somebody else's barbecue. If you are unemployed and more likely to spend the money required to purchase a bag of charcoal on a meal for the family – well, at least you can watch in on the world of *Blue Peter*, where a barbecue is as natural as the middle-class garden in which the 'cooking' is done.

The recipes offered are most interesting, particularly in the light of recent concern over the dietary habits of many of the youth of this country. They are uniformly unhealthy with a high fat and sugar content. The first is for 'nutty burgers' which are unremarkable and, in the manner presented, unattractive. The second is for barbecue baked beans which require the addition of sugar to a product which has already a high sugar content. The third is for a North American invention known as 'S'mores', which consist of two toasted marshmallows sandwiched between chocolate-coated digestive biscuits. Peter Duncan prepares these dishes with Janet. He wears a chef's hat. This is not the image of sacrifice and caring associated with the charity work undertaken by *Blue Peter*. It is the *Blue Peter* of conspicuous middle-class consumption.

This and the previous item act as two misplaced codas which serve only to link the Angelical Voice Choir to the main feature of the programme. They do, however, serve their purpose as mini-vectors of the ideologies which overlap and interweave within the fabric of the show. They are concerned with the comfort of knowing that, in years to come, there *may* be another Torvill and Dean and the solace provided by an imaginary link to a world of barbecues on lawns and the very sweetness of nutty burgers and S'mores. They are not presented as an example of culinary imperialism. Their purpose is to preserve and strengthen our ability to ignore contradictions; to resolve any possible concern about the ideological exports of the United States of America; to preserve our individual and corporate psychic stability.

We are now ready for the introduction of the (apparently) unusual in the form of a story about Prince Lee Boo. The story is introduced to camera by Simon as follows:

'Now if you like true adventures we've got an extraordinary one coming up. Imagine what it would feel like to come to London from a tiny island, thousands of miles away, with no television, film or books to tell you what England was like. Well, 200 years ago, that's what happened to the young Prince of a Pacific island. He came as a visitor to Rotherhithe and Janet has been catching up with his amazing story.'

We are then re-introduced to the story by Janet who is standing near the river at Rotherhithe. She tells us how the people of Rotherhithe still remember Lee Boo's extraordinary story. Just how she or *Blue Peter* managed to ascertain what the 'People of Rotherhithe' think or remember is not clear.

The salient points in the narrative are as follows. In 1783, a boat belonging to the East India Company was shipwrecked and the Captain, Henry Wilson, and his crew found themselves marooned on a tiny Pacific island. The inhabitants were friendly and they eventually built a boat together which took the Captain and his crew on the first leg of the long journey back to England. Prince Lee Boo, at the request of his father, went with them. After many months they arrived in London and the young Prince stayed with the Captain and his family. He went to Rotherhithe Academy and learned to read and write. He was to return to his home one day and teach his people all that he had learned. Unfortunately he caught smallpox, against which he had no resistance, and he died.

It is indeed a most interesting story, but what is much more significant is the deformations and omissions which characterised its telling. It is, like most things which are broadcast on *Blue Peter*, heavily sanitized and littered with significant absences. I intend to identify just a few.

The boat which sank was called the 'Antelope' and belonged to 'the wealthy East India Company.' Indeed it was, and at the expense of millions of the inhabitants of India. These ardent British capitalists grew rich, taking over at one point the whole of Bengal, disrupting Indian society, impoverishing and killing millions. It was *that* East India Company to which the 'Antelope' belonged. India, China, anywhere was ripe for exploitation. Captain Wilson was just one small operative in a large organisation. His individual feelings are less significant historically than the role which he and his like played in subjugating peoples and causing death and suffering in the name of profit.

The portrayal of the islanders is in the best tradition of adventure stories from the days of the British Empire. The crew, we are told, had heard that they were savages. They had 'masses of fuzzy hair' and their bodies were covered with paint. Indeed, they looked a 'fearsome sight.' Not as fearsome, some might say, as a boatload of white imperialists. We are also told of the relief and delight which Captain and crew experienced on finding that the natives were friendly. Captain Wilson made such an impression on the rupack, or ruler, that he was willing to entrust his son to the Captain's care. Leaving aside the wisdom or otherwise of such a move, the narrative is constructed in a manner which makes it very clear that Lee Boo was a lucky Prince to be able to come over and see how 'we' lived. Indeed, as they left in the newly-built craft, with Prince Lee Boo feeling strange in English clothes, the inhabitants of the island chanted at the Captain 'come to us again good Englishman.'

Parts of the story are illustrated by pen and wash drawings. In them Lee Boo becomes increasingly westernised, 'with his interested face, fuzzy hair tied back and his neat clothes.'

'And his patronising narrator,' one is tempted to add.

Once in England, Lee Boo endeared himself to the people of Rotherhithe. He went to Church and quickly learned that 'bad men stay in earth – good men go into sky, become beautiful.' Whether or not he learned anything about women we are not told. The stress is on the way the 'people' of Rotherhithe were taken with this young man. He is portrayed with benevolence as an interesting oddity.

Lee Boo would press money into the hands of an old man in the street, saying that the old man was 'no able to work.' Whilst the East India Company pillages vast sections of the world for profit, Lee Boo and *Blue Peter* teach us a thing or two about charity. One wonders whether Lee Boo put Captain Wilson and his family to shame, or whether they thought to themselves, 'You'll learn, Lee Boo, you'll learn.' *Blue Peter* leaves us in no doubt that Lee Boo was a fine person. But then, he was also one of the 'strangest visitors' Rotherhithe had ever seen.

When the story has been told and Lee Boo has died of smallpox to the accompaniment of a suitably sombre change on the music track, we return to Janet in Rotherhithe. She does not mention the fact that smallpox was not the only disease 'we' foisted upon many peoples who had no immunity or resistance to offer, including influenza and venereal disease. Instead, she shows us a memorial plaque in a Church in Rotherhithe which is dated August 9th, 1783. On it, the crew of the 'Antelope' remember that 'the barbarous people showed us no little kindness.' In other words, they were not barbarous at all. But the contradiction escapes Janet, who moves on to show us the place where Lee Boo is buried. A brief verse is engraved on the bottom of the gravestone. She reads it with us and for us:

> 'Stop reader stop
> Let nature claim a tear
> A Prince of Mine, Lee Boo
> Lies buried here.'

The capital M makes it clear that Lee Boo belongs to more than the people of Rotherhithe. He is also God's. What is not mentioned is that the millions of dead as a result of the exploits of the East India Company could also be considered part of our heritage. But that belongs to a discourse absent from *Blue Peter*. Instead we are told that 'Lee Boo has never been forgotten in Rotherhithe.'

At a time when racist attacks are on the increase, we are told that Rotherhithe is organising a 'Lee Boo Festival' in which several schools will be involved. One can already imagine the drawings of the shipwreck and the 'natives' that will decorate the classroom walls. The ideology of quietism penetrates deeply. There will be no festival in Rotherhithe for Nelson Mandela, nor will the poems of Linton Kwesi Johnson be read to the viewers of *Blue Peter*. There is no room in their discourse for the true adventures recounted in *Dread Beat and Blood*.

The final section of the programme returns to the studio and the Angelical Voice Choir. Peter Duncan tells us that the Lee Boo Festival is something which he is sure would make Lee Boo very happy. It now remains for the story of Lee Boo to be linked with the singing to follow. Simon obliges as follows:

'Now for the hottest of the hot gospellers. Gospel singing has a tradition that goes back almost as far as Lee Boo, 200 years. And I'm not surprised it's so popular – the rhythms and tunes really do cheer you up.'

They *may* if you are a Christian. They may also be interpreted as a desiccated version of what was once a crying out against oppression and a search for salvation which originated with the Blues singers. If you are a Rastafarian you may weep as you watch. But if you are a typical *Blue Peter* viewer, you are constructed so as to appreciate the cheering qualities of the rhythms and tunes. Forget the lyrics. In the words of a song from Viewpoint II,[2] 'Black folks they got rhythm.' One is reminded here of another version of the rhythmic 'potential' of black people in a song sung by Lena Horne for a film by the Cuban film-maker Santiago Alvarez, entitled 'Now.' The words run:

'They all saying we got rhythm,
Let's share some of our rhythm with 'em.'

In these two lines are to be found a celebration of sexuality and joy in living combined with an overt call for revolution. Not a discourse for *Blue Peter*.

The Choir continues with a rendition of a piece from 'a huge repertoire of songs of hope and joy . . . chosen especially for *Blue Peter* – "Lift Him Up"'. It is taken for granted that the viewer will grasp the significance of the title. We are invited, anyway, to concentrate upon rhythm and tune. Just in case we are in any doubt as to the type of response we should be making, there is a shot during the song of the three presenters on their sofa. Their mediation here is almost literally physical. They are bouncing and moving to the rhythm. Simon is ostentatiously manoeuvering his forearm whilst surreptitiously looking around the studio to make sure everything is under control.

When the piece is finished the three presenters burst across in front of the choir with comments such as 'Brilliant,' 'Absolutely brilliant,' and 'You can come round my house every morning and do that.' The comments are as hollow as the patronisation is sincere.

This is further accentuated by Simon's questions about the length of time the choir has been together which was quoted earlier. After a couple of announcements Peter throws his hands high in the air and says evangelically: 'So – see you a week today. Goodbye.' The last word is almost shouted as the rhythm of the organ and percussion begin and the three presenters clap hands and move from foot to foot in a carefully rehearsed closing number entitled 'The Power of God'.

But the programme has had less to do with the power of God than with the power of ideology.

Blue Peter has shown its multi-cultural potential. It has woven together the exploits of an agent of the infamous East India Company with a deliberately romanticised story of a young black Prince. This has been linked in a most tenuous manner with the music of the Angelical Voice Choir. There *is*, however, a common thread running through the programme. The blacks represented are in no sense a threat to anyone. Prince Lee Boo wanted to learn 'our' ways so that he could 'educate' his people. The Angelical Voice Choir is, in the end, interested in saving souls. Their business is with another world. You will not find them on the Front Line.[3] Lee Boo can be patronised and placed easily in the warped historiography of *Blue Peter*. The evangelical strength of the Choir can be utilised as a means of patting black people on the head for being good rhythmic citizens with 'Christian' values.

Such a programme is an obstacle to the extension of knowledge and a means of closing off alternative possibilities of thought. It is a vector of true bourgeois ideology and its membrane of stylistic devices seems at first impermeable. But once the discourses of *Blue Peter* are reconstructed from the obfuscating pseudo-rhetoric employed by its presenters, it can be identified as riddled with contradictions, racist, sexist and reactionary.

Roland Barthes once wrote that, in order to live to the full the contradiction of our time it may be necessary to make sarcasm the condition of truth. To which we must perhaps add now the need for analytical invective as an antidote to the functionings of ideology.

Notes

1. It is worth noting here that in November, 1982, BARB produced a top ten of children's programmes which included only one 'children's' programme. *Blue Peter* was rated tenth. The report also indicated that, whilst the viewing audience for *Blue Peter* was 5 million, only 1.5 million of these viewers were children.
2. Broadcast by Thames Television as part of the 'English Programme' for secondary schools.
3. The name by which the central areas of conflict between the police and population of Brixton became known. It centred on Railton Road.

Bill Lewis

TV Games: People as Performers

Television's myths become most visible when television steps outside its normal practices. So what could be more unusual, and revealing, than a penetration of this seamlessly professional medium by non-professional, non-expert performers? Yes, it's game show time. The curtain of mystery is pulled back and the Public (it could be you or me) is permitted a few short, sharp, seconds of stardom (providing, that is, we can treat the game as a bit of fun and don't really need the prizes). It's a curious role, that of game show contestant, for it contains an ambiguity which illustrates television's own uncertainty over how and where s/he should be positioned. Let's call them 'spectator/participants', then: 'participants' because they're clearly necessary to ensure the action of the game, but also 'spectators' because they watch the game and, frequently, demonstrate links with the studio audience by applauding the game's prestigious features.

The physical positioning of spectator/participant within various game show spaces indicates elements of control within hierarchical structures. Thus, the spectator/participant acknowledges homage to the perceived importance of the event by dressing formally. Further, a common icon of these games is the desk behind which s/he sits or stands in the game's initial stages. The successful player gains the right to move from the desk to another playing space and with it the right to play for greater rewards. This sign of success reinforces complex and powerful myths of social and educational mobility. Emphasising television's own sense of self-importance, the supreme ascription of success is the right to space in a subsequent programme ('Can-you-come-back-next-week?'). The physical positioning of the host is significant, too, in defining the position of spectator/participant for, typically, his (and I use that pronoun deliberately) status is marked by freedom of movement. Again, typically, after opening shots of contestants he is shown walking onto the set, to applause. He may initiate and close brief, socially-placing conversations with contestants and may demonstrate his own status by moving around the set to address them. But his own subordinacy to the game is marked by his return to a defined position from which to set the tasks. Further, the authority of the game space, and his authority as agent of that space, is asserted by his right to lead the most successful to further, but deferred, participation. His role, then, is continually to sanction the ineffability of the game and the unquestioned worth of its key constituents – prizes, contestants and tasks – doing so by calling on the legitimised myths of society. Thus, of prizes: 'After the break we'll be back with *Double Money* and *Big Money*,' '£180 *and* a five-inch colour television – isn't that wonderful!'. Of contestants:

Q: You're a fine upstanding chap by the look of you. What do you do for a living?'
A: I'm a policeman.'

And of the tasks: 'if Andy does as well as that you'll be in the Big Money.' Even failure becomes absorbed into this hegemony of success so that the game is all: 'The microwave doesn't go to Paul, but nevertheless it's a very good start to the game,' 'You got four (%), not bad;' or even, when the consequences of failure can no longer be resisted,

Q: Hope you've had a nice day.
A: Yes, I've had a lovely time.'

Jeopardy, *Odd One Out* and *The Pyramid Game* all share with *Mastermind* a dependence on the assumed authority of shared cultural expectations and practices in order to motivate the plot and, thus, to ascribe rewards. Unlike *Mastermind*, though, but like *Family Fortunes*, their settings work to celebrate specifically financial rewards available through competition. The opening titles of *The Pyramid Game*, for example, show vivid optical patterns interspersed with the '£' symbol; *Odd One Out* opens with a close up of 'last week's winner' whilst a voice over tells how much s/he won; after an opening establishing shot of the set, the second sequence of *Family Fortunes* shows, to studio applause, the variety of consumer durables offered as 'this week's prizes', creating the extraordinary event of an entire studio audience applauding a rotary ironer; a small screen at the front of the spectator/participants' desk in *Jeopardy* shows continuously each individual's current winnings; while a striking image of *The Pyramid Game* shows a huge illuminated triangle (pyramid) which flashes behind the game space. It is divided into areas each titled with an amount of money from '£25' to '£150', the lesser sums being at the triangle's base. Incandescent above the apex is the top prize, picked out in lights, '£1000'.

    Mastermind may seem, in some senses, exceptional, in its rather genteel rejection of overt consumerist vulgarities and foregrounding of a self-effacing quest for learning, yet it, too, offers a rich ore for analysis. The programme's homage to knowledge is apparent from its university setting and that quasi-tutorial engagement of Magnusson and contestant. To these might be added the first image of the contestants, seated front centre surrounded by their peers, the elite position in an image recalling the collegiate photograph. This setting and its connotations mark the formality of the event, as do the slow, deliberate and ritualised movements between chair and audience. That spotlit chair, isolated at the end of a catwalk in the centre of the arena, the surrounding darkness and the slow zoom through three camera positions during the interrogation, all serve to reify the contestant and, by association, the knowledge that s/he bears. Magnusson's placing in *Mastermind* is significant, too. Unlike all other game show hosts his position is not central, but left of screen. He, and his assistant, continue the circle of peers which is completed by the inscribed presence of the viewer. His greyness, age and gravity signify wisdom and scholarship, but his personal status is reduced by his placement in the circle, a shape which symbolises the surrounding and apparently united culture. From his position in the circle he voices what is represented as the collective knowledge of that culture to the contestant who is at once celebrant and initiate. Like other game show hosts, his role, too, is subordinate, an acolyte at a secular celebration of, this time, the rite of knowledge. Success or failure of individual celebrants is immaterial: each week there will be a winner and the myth confirmed.

Having offered some comment on myths of wealth and knowledge as positioning axes within game shows, I wish to consider one further axis of positioning, that third determinant of patriarchal power: sex. Given our culture's habit of linking economic success with sexual success, it is perhaps hardly surprising that the game show, a form which places great emphasis on the dominant norms of a consumerist culture, should both adopt and confirm society's sexual myths. Women game show 'hosts' have been conspicuous by their absence, appearing, instead, as the attractive assistant in a subordinate role to the questioner. The 'hosts', then, are male, white and well-groomed, with short hair and expensive suits. Occasionally a non-RP accent may be permissible, but only if the host (e.g., Max Bygraves, Paul Daniels) has already been ascribed celebrity status in another field. Their possession of the knowledge necessary both to play and win the game assimilates them into a powerful system of patriarchal authority consisting of immensely convoluted male/ middle-class/white/knowledge/television/consumerism/important/ domination/objectivity equations. From this position they deploy sexual mores to address spectator/participants in ways clearly irrelevant to the micro-structures of the game's mechanics but central to the macro-structures of the game's ideology. Fellow males are treated with affable deference, even respect, as women become objects of studied flirtation or butts of sexist jokes. Thus, the appellations 'my love' or 'dear' too frequent to catalogue. Or the revelation of one lady's occupation at Heathrow Airport being the excuse for a sustained series of innuendos on the theme of frisking.

The myths of television, then, actively work to confer a contemporary *droit de seigneur* on the male host, and simultaneously legitimise this safe sexuality. 'Safe' because public, an aspect of his interpersonal licence as celebrity, an aspect of the game show as closed event, and because conducted with apparent audience approval. Again, *Mastermind* seems to be something of an exception to this. The image of Magnusson cracking raunchy sexist one-liners to the rough guffaws of a studio audience seems an unlikely one. I would argue, though, that notions of sexual positioning are not irrelevant to an understanding of that game's ideological work. Rather, it would seem that *Mastermind*, with its foregrounding of objectivity, rationality and certainty, and its consequent erasure of emotion, intuition and non-verbal communication, has adopted a discourse of patriarchal authority to which the sexuality of both women and men contestants becomes completely subsumed, and within which they are positioned.

The ubiquitous game show, then, occupies a space in the mythologies of television which has failed to attract the kind of critical attention which it undoubtedly deserves. By revealing the television medium atypically assimilating members of the public into its signifying practices, it offers a valuable model for analysis. Further, in that process of assimilation is demonstrated vividly the larger ideological work of the mass media: persistently concealing pervasive social inequalities behind an unquestioning celebration of highly selective cultural and material values.

Sean Cubitt

Top of the Pops: the Politics of the Living Room

Every Thursday evening at about 7.30 several million people see their TV screens explode. If it's Thursday night, it's *Top of the Pops*. But after that momentary ecstasy, and its promise of a programme whose energy will blow your screen apart, it's business as usual. For the last twenty years, adolescents and young adults have regularly switched to *Top of the Pops*, knowing that the chance of seeing rock-and-roll rebellion is less than likely, but still titillating enough to keep them watching. The experience of the past counts for little: the *Top of the Pops* viewer lives in a present of eternal optimism. Songs are never played on their way down the charts, only on their way up. And the knowledge that large parts of the programme will be taken up by performers of minimal interest (novelty act/crooner/hype band, etc.); that the formula will be as it always is; that ambitious young people will ogle the camera and rich pop stars will preen themselves in absurd costumes – none of this matters. The *Top of the Pops* viewer lives in a state of permanent hope. Unlike radio, or even other TV pop shows, *Top of the Pops* lacks even a short-term memory for pop.

There are no 'Golden Oldies', no résumés of careers here. Simply thraldom to the charts. Hence, quite apart from the consistency of its ratings, the importance of the programme for the industrial side of the record business. Young teenagers, the crucial market for pop singles, do tend to be at home for that early evening slot, and can confidently be expected to be interested in 'the latest'. Not for them an education in the origins and history of their music, its sociology, its links with big business, cultural nationalism or the politics of race, gender or age. Even the technology – apparent in shots that include other cameras or the studio lighting galleries – is put in the foreground only to be glamourised. As a technique it seems to offer an inside view of the production of the programme, an effect developed in modernist art at the beginning of the century and now widely used by advertisers, and by the makers of pop videos. Yet while it boasts of an 'honesty' (and thus a kind of accountability) to the viewer, it finally shows only in order to take away again. The pictures of camera operators and lighting bars themselves become images from the glamorous world of the stars. Like the images of the stars, they offer the illusion of intimacy, whilst simultaneously maintaining an unbridgeable gap between the viewer and the star. That is how glamour works.

Top of the Pops' problem is to contain the larger-than-life world of pop in the little box in the corner of the living room. Hampered by the early evening slot, the BBC has to censor groups and videos, most notoriously the Sex Pistols and Frankie Goes To Hollywood. Add to this the poor quality of the speakers on most television sets and the result is a sanitising of pop music's sexuality and rebellion, a miniaturisation of its torment, thrills and excesses. Yet clearly there is still something there to draw the young viewers back to the screen again.

One attraction, surely, is just to see what those Great Names look like. For most of this century, the major circulation of music was on disc, tape and radio – all purely audio media. Around them grew a wealth of secondary material from fan clubs, magazines, films and newspapers to satisfy the urgent curiosity of the fans as to what these people, whose songs could touch them so deeply, actually looked like.

What was more logical than to put pop idols on to the small screen? But how to film them? Without cataloguing all of the shifts in style over the years since the programme first came on the air, the one key element that has become central to the *Top of the Pops* visual style is the singer gazing lovingly/threateningly into the camera, right into your living room. It gives the show an air of actually communicating something with some degree of urgency, and it does give viewers a rare chance to look at boys with the kind of sexual interest usually reserved for pictures of girls. Is this how boys (or girls) should look? How are the bright young things of London carrying themselves this week? It's not just fashions, it's the production of role models for youngsters in the first flush of youth, getting through the painful process of puberty and fine-tuning their future personalities. It's a time of very genuine emotional upheaval, an upheaval most adults have to joke about, and so one that requires a closing of ranks among adolescents.

And that, of course, is the rationale behind the other classic *Top of the Pops* shots, the camera moving either in to or out from close up, to bring us all into the midst of the dancers. This is a very curious movement. It opens up a conflict between the shot's 'cinematic' function, of drawing the viewer into the ' filmic' space, and the strictures of the domestic viewing space – which militate against identification in any traditional sense. Its purpose is to draw us into the magical community of *Top of the Pops*, into that wonderful world without parents. But if the camera draws us in, the family pulls us out. Real parents are always likely to burst in on the dream of community and disrupt it. Having your family sit in on your emotional life and pass unfavourable comments on the object(s) of your desire is doubly unpleasant because much of the business of romance, which occupies so much of the deodorised realm of *Top of the Pops* is about leaving home and setting up shop with someone new. It's a fragile, delicate moment, one that *Top of the Pops* constantly, if obliquely, addresses through its dancers, its videos and its singers. We're invited to identify, not with the singers, but with the dancers, with their community, and it's an identification that's all too open to the politics of the living room.

In some ways the pop video has changed *Top of the Pops* quite radically. Acts can now have a measure of control over their presentation, and the production values are startlingly higher than for ordinary pop TV (£15,000 is often quoted as the average price for three minutes, though the rumoured cost of Michael Jackson's 'Thriller' video was over $1 million). But for all their expense and all their variety, running the gamut from German silent films through advertising's peculiar brand of surrealism, to the rather tedious concert footage they first arose from, videos don't in general break any of the moulds of classic TV. The main difference is simply their brevity and the consequent speed at which their images flash by. But clearly they offer a range and variety to the programme that it would never achieve any other way. 'The world is our oyster,' they seem to say, with their flashy images of yachts and surfers, but it's a world where the excess of emotion – the excess of soul from Bessie Smith to the Shangri-La's – has become an excess of consumer goods, of holidays, boats and Bacardis.

When the bland young boys crinkle their eyebrows and twist their mouths into the conventional signs of authentic emotion, something about television stops you from believing them totally. Because they are so small, because the amplification is so weak, because they are in your living room. Curiously, *Top of the Pops* doesn't make the music more immediate; it mediates the music, putting us at one remove from it. And still I'll be turning on next Thursday, to see if the cathode ray tube will finally explode into a million fragments from the sheer energy of pop songs that break the mould, disintegrating the already uneasy world of teen anguish and romance.

Richard Paterson

Fragments of Neil: Entertainment & Political Leadership

Political parties have perceived the importance of television as a medium of persuasion since the late fifties and early sixties. Television, as it has developed in this country, has been tied, as if by an umbilical cord, to consumerism and the privatisation of pleasure. This has had important effects in altering the parameters of political discourse, which are now firmly wedded to the agency of advertising so crucial to the consumer-based economy. With image building now very important, there has been an inevitable impact on the 'message' of leadership.

However, television itself is not some unitary form into which politics has been inserted. Television is fragmented by programme type, addressing different audiences, employing different modes of address, as it seeks to entertain, inform or educate the viewer. It represents and presents images of class, gender and race. It mediates (some would assert that it even sets) political agendas. Into this television world the fragments of a political leader's appearances have to be slotted, as part of the effort to convince the electorate of his or her suitability for office.

What, then, of the new Labour Party leader Neil Kinnock, elected at the Labour Party conference in October, 1983, just four months after Labour's disastrous election defeat by the Conservatives' well-oiled marketing machine? The choice as leader of a man who appears always articulate and shrewd – an almost perfect 'media politician' – has had significant consequences in a re-evaluation of strategies by the Labour Party machine.

The public always has to 'read' the television image of the leader from the many representations available. Of course, some preconception of what a party leader is and does always exists. But for Neil Kinnock, achieving recognition as a potential Prime Minister was complicated by his lack of ministerial experience, and his earlier media performances – which included the famous (and perhaps ill-judged) riposte to a heckler about 'guts at Goose Green' in the TVS programme *The South Decides*, during the election campaign. Party leaders have to use all available means in the many fragments of their television appearances to establish their authority, credibility and trustworthiness – to create a television persona. Neil Kinnock's need was to adapt his acknowledged television skills to overcome his handicaps, and to set a new agenda for the perception of Labour politics.

The television image of 'Neil Kinnock' is constructed by the audience out of all the leader's various public appearances. Throughout the text which is comprised by these fragmentary appearances Kinnock's goals are constantly repeated. His principal objective is defined as winning power within the accepted framework of party politics.

However, this self-presentation is invariably viewed and read differently by the various sub-sectors of the TV audience. Despite any politician's attempts to alter perceptions and to confirm a particular reading of their 'message', television necessarily offers a plurality of meanings which can never be fully controlled. Moreover, politics on television, whilst overtly 'about' principles and beliefs (the discourse of party politics) has to face the added complication of needing to appeal to the electorate via the modes of presentation most appropriate to television – e.g. that of 'personalities'. Problems of both 'principle' and 'personality' must therefore be successfully negotiated. Following on from Margaret Thatcher's frequent appearances on chat shows (the *Jimmy Young Show* on radio, Michael Aspel's show and *A Plus 4* on television), Neil Kinnock, too, has adopted a strategy of appearing in 'entertainment' slots in order to speak to the widest possible audience – thus his pop video with Tracy Ullman and his rendering of *Singing in the Rain* outside a meeting of the Welsh TUC.

As John Wright, who ran the advertising campaign for the Labour Party in the 1983 election, has said, 'I think that one of the things we have to learn from the last election is unless we use television in every way, and every form of television better, we will suffer, as we did against the Tories.' (At Guildford, October, 1983. See below).

The use by the Conservative Party of modern marketing techniques in the 1983 General Election led them 'to keep constantly in mind what was concerning people and to answer the questions in peoples' minds.' (Christopher Lawson at South East Arts/BFI event 'Marketing the Leader', October, 1983, Guildford.) The Labour Party's corresponding move into the 'electronic age' has been completed with Kinnock's selection (or perhaps revisited, considering Harold Wilson's legendary adeptness at using television), but the tension between marketing a product and maintaining principles has never been so acute. The shop window is now to be arranged for consumption, using opinion surveys to that end. It is reported that the party machine will continually take opinion surveys and apply the information to those areas where Labour should legitimately be seen to be campaigning – but with a much higher profile, and more clearly led, by its leader.

But the leader appears in fragments on television. Mostly this is in the news, then in occasional interviews at length in current affairs programmes, then wherever else an appearance is possible and considered advantageous. The problem is whether the fragments make a unitary whole. And what of satirical representations, such as *Spitting Images'* use of the famous fall on the beach at Brighton just before the leadership election in its opening titles (the 'puppet's' string is cut), or the skulking Luck and Flaw figure in the Shadow cabinet meetings. For some this is a trivialisation of politics, but such a view is based on a limited perception of the 'political'. What television repetition provides is a constant flow of accounting via interviewers and commentators, and selling by party leaders; not exactly accountability, but a view of the bare cupboards of much political debate which either inures, or in a more optimistic scenario, creates a context of truthfulness where conviction is more important than cosmetics. Perhaps the Thatcher victory owed more to the electorate's perception of a leader's (and Party's) belief in a programme of action, than the marketing of a leader. After all, marketing the Prime Minister is no new phenomenon in British politics, having previously been adopted by the Conservatives in 1959 (cf. Andrew Gamble *The Conservative Nation*). Certainly, political debate on public issues in the private domain of television viewing has created a national space for politics, in which politicians can speak directly to the nation. The elision of class and other divisions which is encouraged by this idea of a unitary nation is, of course, open to exploitation since there is in fact no necessary unity, but the Labour Party seems not to know how to mobilise this potential. The fragments of Neil have made a poor 'substitute Margaret' so far.

Kinnock's image 'in extenso' was conveyed most clearly in a *Newsnight* interview in July 1984, at the end of his first parliamentary session as leader. The interview was preceded by a look back at his performance in Labour's year of recovery, on the same day that he had achieved victory at the National Executive Committee for his views on the reselection of MPs (later rejected at the 1984 Labour Party Annual Conference). Kinnock's victory was argued by Betty Boothroyd MP to demonstrate his leadership qualities. 'It's what leaders do', she replied when asked about Kinnock's wisdom in taking a gamble with his authority in the party. Kinnock's leadership (described by the *Newsnight* commentary as offering relief and a new hope in 1983 as he looked towards the possibilities of the future and turned his back on defeat) has been seen as having the advantage of 'an authority and unity as leader which few leaders (of the Labour Party) have had in recent times'. Certainly, as *Newsnight* commented, it was widely argued that the Labour Party realised it was now time to focus on external political campaigning after five years of internal wrangles.

In commenting on Kinnock's leadership, the programme asserted in its commentary that Kinnock had become accepted as a credible leader – humorous, likeable and human – even though some still felt he was lightweight, or calculating. It was felt that he may have had more style than substance, especially when up against Margaret Thatcher in Parliament, with her nine years of experience as party leader. On the miners' strike, his belated identification with the workers had, on the one hand, been seen as lacking conviction and on the other, confirmed a (Conservative) view of him as Arthur Scargill's poodle. In the European elections he had been presented in Presidential style, which had offended some. The montage of fragments of Neil Kinnock on television left the impression of a leader who had yet to achieve authority, but who had set the ball rolling again for the Labour Party, and was trying to keep its electoral chances open by not treading too far outside known territory.

The *Newsnight* interview by John Tusa was set up around questions of performance, authority and credibility – one version of the Kinnock story to date. Neil Kinnock, able to use the montage as his starting point, attempted in the interview to assert his qualities as leader, asserting his priority over the interviewer on one occasion, but in the main answering the questions, even though sometimes deflected by Tusa's interruptions.

Television as image maker and political broker here becomes tied to its oral qualities. Power of speech and associated kinesic markers take priority. First there is an assumption of leadership: 'I must speak up for people I stand for... it would be less than honest not to'. Then a criticism of government for not using its existing power – 'I want the government to govern. I wish they'd start to do it. Then the country would be in a much better situation. If they can't do it, they should shift aside. We'll lead and we'll govern.'

Tusa questioned Kinnock closely about the miners' strike and the rebuffs he had received – first to his call for a national ballot, then to his condemnation of violence on the picket lines. Tusa also referred to Kinnock's subsequent appearance on a platform with Arthur Scargill, saying there was no alternative but to fight and that Mrs. Thatcher must be denied victory. In response, Kinnock turned directly to the question of *power*. His own goal was clearly that of getting power – and it is with reference to this central objective that all his actions and comments become understandable. As he remarked, 'a leader cannot be asked to fulfil responsibilities for which I have no power,' ... and 'until I am Prime Minister there will be no additional power.' Both these remarks confirm Robert Harris' comment in *The Making of Neil Kinnock* (1984) '.... for Kinnock politics is not about striking heroic stances: it is about power.'

These various observations about Neil Kinnock on television, using the particular example of a *Newsnight* interview, lead to some tentative conclusions. Political discourse exists outside television, but the generally acknowledged centrality of television in national debate necessitates particularly close attention to TV performance by a party leader. The perception of a leader on TV, however, is formed by the aggregation of many fragmentary appearances. There are two levels of action. The 'real world' of politics in which political actors act; and relatedly, but separate, the television representation, using modes of entertainment and personality appeal alongside the discourse of politics.

For a leader, the fragments in different registers (from still image over speeches in Parliament, to video cameo, to interviews in current affairs programmes, to satirical sketches by others) come together to engage both the discourse of politics, for which the goal of power is central for Neil Kinnock, and TV discourses based on personality. In the disjointed world of television the leader is open to inspection. But when personality seems as important as the domain of the political, how to relate politics to the consumer becomes a dominant concern. If this path is followed the politicians seem to need to aggregate the biggest audience available for their message and to parade themselves, just as advertisers do.

Certainly the continual attempt to achieve the common touch (for instance, via Neil Kinnock's video appearance) to talk to *all* the people, using television's own pre-existing means of audience aggregation, fits in with the consumer oriented world of TV. But, somehow, there is also an ever-present threat for the leader of being revealed by television's interrogations as being without substance. Personality can achieve much, but the sideshow of politics can always strike back. Keeping a credible stance and maintaining an acceptable persona can be difficult. The fragments, too, need to cohere in some kind of unity. The actions of the leader in his ongoing struggle for power (in the 'real world') need to stay in step with the accumulating fragments of the leader in the TV world. Not to achieve coherence of this kind leads to a dissonance which will be damaging in full view of an increasingly teleliterate electorate. The marketing dreamland of television can then turn into a nightmare for the politician.

Bruce Carson

Romantic Perfection:
the Torvill and Dean Story

'Nottingham's favourite son and daughter', Torvill and Dean, have
come to represent the perfect couple. They're a sort of home-grown
Fred Astaire and Ginger Rogers on ice. Television has transformed
their performance into a musical spectacle of romance and success.
Commentators describe them as possessing 'a magical chemistry',
and of being 'a marriage of extraordinary talents'. Such a language of
romantic coupledom reveals how their story is as much about 'Will
they, won't they settle down together?' as 'Will they win?', their
sporting achievements being projected onto some future domesticity.
The fact that no one can guarantee a happy ending to the story gives
an added frisson of pleasure to those millions of viewers who are
absorbed in this fantasy of perfection. However, it is also a pleasure
that serves to reinforce the status quo.

Whether or not 'Chris and Jayne' get their act together, both on
or off the ice, is part of the tension and uncertainty that specialist
sports commentators are itching to exploit. The enigma of their
personal relationship is placed at the forefront in interviews. For
example, Barry Davies, in his politest BBC manner, wants to know
whether all this visual eroticism is left frozen on the ice or finds its
expression in off-duty hours as well. So, he asks, 'Can I finally bring
you back to the public, the British public, who are slightly concerned
that they won't see enough of you when you go professional. They're
looking for an end to the fairytale, aren't they? You'll probably tell
me not this week. Do you foresee a happy end to the fairytale at some
time for Messrs. Torvill and Dean?' With a not very subtle mixture of
understatement and a nervous answering of his own question, Barry
probes for the reality of their private lives. Like *Come Dancing*, ice
dance is also a celebration of the traditional couple, the basis of which
is an image of harmony. So, he feels that with all that 'togetherness'
there must be some romantic involvement. However, in this process
of media inquisition the inequality that this coupledom symbolises is
ignored. It is seen to be 'natural' for men to be the dominant partners,
and women the objects of sexual display.

Meanwhile, over on ITV's *World of Sport*, Dickie Davis is asking
'Do you think you can be beaten?' This dialogue of topdog and

underdog in sport is part of a wider view that sees 'competition' as being a 'normal' part of society. Since schooldays we've all been fed on a language that sees success or failure in intellectual or sporting life as being in the hands of each person, irrespective of social background. In a similar vein, Barry Davies is also reassuring us 'that success even of Olympic proportions' hasn't changed Torvill and Dean, they're still the shy young police cadet and insurance clerk they once were. This image of off-ice 'ordinariness' makes them appear just like ourselves. Yet, their Cinderella-like transformation from 'ordinary' young people into graceful skaters also helps to confirm their celebrity status. As stars from a conventional social background, their success helps to reinforce the myth that our society is based solely on personal achievement and not on privilege.

However much the audience identifies with this populist stardom, it is the spectacle of Torvill and Dean's performances that is central to viewers' pleasure. It's an enjoyment that owes as much to their display as to the drama of the final result. As they move across the ice to the music of Ravel or Rimsky-Korsakov their gestures and movements express a powerful sexuality. It's an eroticism that indulges viewers' fantasies of domination or submission.

In the *paso doble* routine they explore the theme of the matador fighting a bull. The matador emphatically asserts the dominance and arrogance of the male, both as bullfighter and as dancing partner. During this routine Jayne Torvill symbolises the bullfighter's cape, remaining impassive while she is flung dramatically around the ice, to end up finally at Christopher Dean's feet. In Alan Weeks' immortal words, 'Jayne is on the ice, the crowd are on their feet'. Such an overt display of masculine power is in opposition to the more feminine approach of *Bolero*. This balletic dance has a romantic theme based around the passionate yearning and tragic death of two young lovers. During its performance each dancer expresses a mutual surrender that is in stark contrast to the aggressive choreography of the earlier *paso doble*. The visual power of the *Bolero* routine adds further fuel to speculation about their personal relationship off the ice. Like a 'Mills and Boon' romance, the themes of domination and surrender create an image of the ideal couple audiences find so compelling.

However, the television portrayal is as much about what is concealed from, as what is revealed on, viewers' screens. The visual eroticism of Torvill and Dean's routines, with their themes of domination or surrender, are never referred to by commentators. Instead, their performances are discussed in terms of the drama of success and failure. This is witnessed by the fact that any minor slip-up becomes instant national news, as with Jayne Torvill's infamous 'hand on the floor' incident. Old faithfuls like Alan Weeks are telling us what we can see and hear already, 'Look at that crowd in the background, everyone is standing, the commentators in the box are standing and applauding.' With a 'Wish you were here' sense of community, Alan evokes national pride in our couple's individual success with the observation, 'No wonder those Union Jacks are waving. That was absolutely superb,' the final accolade being a statistical confirmation of their perfection: 'Oh, my goodness! They've done it again, nine sixes for presentation, they are astounding!'

Paradoxically, ice dance is about harmony as well as intense competition. References are also made to the routines' 'aesthetic' qualities. These are usually analysed in terms of music, styles of dress, dance techniques, (and in Torvill and Dean's case 'romance'). Such comments place the sport firmly in the area of cultural values that are traditionally thought of as 'feminine'. This is in contrast to the predominance of masculine sporting values that emphasize such virtues as toughness, aggression and achievement. Thus, after the drama of a 'World Championship', Dickie Davis tells Torvill and Dean 'that little girls have been crying to get in to see you'. The real implication of this statement is that any 'little boy' wouldn't have been seen within 50 miles of the stadium. If commentators skate around all that sublimated sexuality, then their language also fails to explore the images of masculinity and femininity that Torvill and Dean represent.

Jayne Torvill's image is based around the good-looking wholesomeness of the girl next door. It fits the 'perfect' image of femininity in our society, that is youthful, slender and boyish. On the other hand, the man's role is seen as a supportive one within the dance couple. Hence, Christopher Dean's 'gentlemanly' image is of a man who is honest, decent and capable, but with an artistic flair that transforms him on the ice into an English Prince Charming. As a couple their displays together exude a high degree of sexuality. However, in all sport there is a reluctance by commentators to discuss bodily display, particularly in the case of the male body. Yet sport is the one area where men's bodies are constantly on view. However, ice dance conforms to the conventional picture of male and female sexuality, in that individuals are viewed from within the confines of the heterosexual couple; in this way Christopher Dean acts as the pivot for displaying Jayne Torvill's figure to the male gaze. In contrast to this, his own attraction to a sport that 'feminizes' the male dancer is never discussed outside of the couple. Ultimately, any discussion of their sexuality is concealed by commentary on the 'competitive' or 'aesthetic' dimensions that operate within the sport.

What is striking about the long-term fantasies of romance and success that underlie Torvill and Dean's story is that behind the glamour and glitter of their star performances lies an essential 'Englishness'. As a couple, their quiet, modest and unassuming office personas reinforce what are perceived as the English virtues of hard-work, levelheadedness and fair play. They exhibit a cool professionalism in response to any media prying into their relationship which contrasts vividly with all the repressed passion of their dancing. This further helps to deepen the mystery surrounding their personal lives. Unlike Prince Charles and Lady Di they are ordinary rather than privileged stars. This increases audience identification with their lower middle-class success story. It is an entirely appropriate story for a conservative era that has reasserted the values of 'competitiveness' as a patriotic ingredient to the English way of life. Yet, ironically, their financial support from Nottingham City Council makes them as much the offspring of the social democratic Welfare State as any privatised dreamland. Not that this matters, for this television folk-tale of honest endeavour and romantic perfection reflects a culture where everyone is supposed to find their 'natural' position in life, regardless of their social origins.

John Corner

Olympic Myths: the Flame, the Night and the Music

Television doesn't so much 'cover' sporting events as use them as the raw material for the construction of an altogether different and increasingly ambitious kind of spectacle – that of televised sport.

Here, as in many other areas of activity regularly attracting 'coverage', it is useful right from the start to understand the word 'televised' to mean something like 'having been changed by the processes of televisation', rather than to mean simply '*on* television'. By thinking of it thus as a term indicating a processed state (compare it with 'pulverised', perhaps, or 'homogenised') and not as an innocent equivalent of 'screened' or 'broadcast', we can at least hope to get some critical purchase upon our experience as viewers.

This being achieved, a key question for the critical viewer becomes – according to what technical and professional recipes did a given piece of televisation get done? Or, in this case, how do the production teams of the TV industry fashion the characteristic features of televised sport from the kinds of ordinary sport which one might see for oneself at a football ground or an athletics stadium?

I think that a good deal of what goes on in their activities can be seen as contributing to the creation of a special kind of perspective. This might be called a perspective of *celebratory seeing*. Through it, a multiple and often intimate visual rendering of sporting action is both organised into the space of the screen for the possession of the steady gaze, and also linked to a soundtrack from which the viewer is prompted and stimulated.

In its visual aspects, such a perspective extensively exploits the medium's capacities for maintaining several viewpoints, for close-ups, 'action replays', freeze-frames and the editing together of 'highlights'. Here the enormous pleasure granted by the facility of *repetition* (whether in 'action replay' format or not) is of crucial importance. It seems to carry with it a heady, magical feeling almost of *having the event happen again* (Dalglish's goal, Coe's kick to the tape), rather than of the watching of a recording.

In its non-visual aspects, the perspective is greatly aided by exclamatory styles of commentary and of 'anchorman' presentation. It also seems increasingly reliant on the use of music to cue viewers into getting the most intense experience possible from watching its images.

If we look briefly at some of the 'stock' sequences from the BBC's 1984 Olympics programming, I think we can see a number of the above devices in quite advanced stages of development and combination. And to considerable celebratory effect.

Music was a key element in the BBC's operation right from the start, following its decision to use the title music from the highly popular film *Chariots of Fire* as the theme for all its Olympics programmes ('That music *says* Olympics, it says British success,' commented BBC TV's Head of Sport).

In this economical way the movie's determinedly patriotic construction of 'Olympicality' within a kind of forcefield of sentiments about national character, the spirituality of hard exercise and the cleanliness and idiosyncratic charm of earlier chapters in our sporting history, was coupled to the images and sounds to be transmitted from Los Angeles. As viewers, our celebration of the processed present was to take its cue from an already celebrated, processed past.

Moreover, the BBC's use of the *Chariots* tune did not serve merely to evoke memories of the film's characters and events. It also installed as central to the programming a particular way of representing sport, one grounded in the technologically-given option of *slow-motion.*

This was so because the expressive possibilities afforded by showing athletics sequences in slow-motion constitute the film's primary formal idea; an idea pursued by its director with an imprudent persistence. Vangelis's now-famous title score is clearly designed to accompany this kind of footage. The theme begins with a pulsing synthesiser bass line (the sound of the life-force itself? athletical heartbeats?) which is then overlaid by a heavier and less rapid drum rhythm (a 'slow-motion' breathing cycle?). We hear a series of stately horn calls and then the main tune – a wistfully phrased piano sequence in relaxed tempo – is played and repeated over the rhythms. Finally, an orchestra takes up a related but more expansive second tune.

The standard opening of the BBC's programmes was a mixture of film and graphics arranged so as to match the movements and mood of this music as felicitously as possible.

Heralded by a sunburst in a clear blue sky, slow-motion shots of past Olympic champions appeared in sequence, 'heads and shoulders' within a circular inset on the blue. Though either on film or videotape and, in some cases, of quite recent origin, the images were sepia-tinted like old photographs. Still against the blue background, a graphics sequence followed, depicting bronze classical columns growing down from the rings of the Olympic emblem. Across the bottom of these columns passed the shadow of a torch-bearer, running in slow-motion across and off the screen. This was 'wiped' to reveal a full-screen sepia shot of Carl Lewis in action, the tint turning slowly up to full colour, thus beginning a further series of shots (more slow-motion) of present international stars. These were updated at points throughout the fortnight so as to remove from the pantheon those who were no longer fitted for the celebratory gaze (e.g., goodbye Alan Wells) and to insert new footage of those who were. The image faded to sepia on the last of these, 'wiping' back to graphics showing the shadow of the runner again, returning across the screen against the background now, not of columns, but of the L.A. Olympics logo.

In a final graphics sequence the camera zoomed upwards towards the Olympic flame tower on top of the L.A. stadium gateway. As the theme music moved into a new passage via a pronounced drumbeat, flames burst out from the bowl at the tower's tip. Through these flames the opening shot of each edition's coverage was established.

Given this thoroughly integrated set of elements, this instance of TV's rhetorical combination of sound and image, I think it's first of all interesting to consider just how slow-motion works on the viewer when, as here and in *Chariots*, it's used outside of the analytic context of the 'action replay'. What it generates, perhaps, is not only a visual lyricism (one which incidentally, at its worst, appears to risk the aesthetic banalities of a 'poetry in motion'). There is also, through the change of speed, a *displacing* of the athletes from 'normal time' into a realm of unreality (in feature films, slow-motion often indicates the time of memory or the time of dream), where, floating freely through their physical routines in all their excellence, they offer an image which can provide a focus, a gathering point, for sporting ideals and myths. Of course, this effect is much helped by the necessary removal of all live ('actuality') sound from the recording. Furthermore, the relative stillness of the slow-motion shot, uncluttered by soundtrack information, though possibly accompanied by music, may permit us to contemplate the *person*, and, as conveyed by the face, the *personal effort*, at least as much as the action or the larger event. There seems to be more than a touch of the 'moving icon' about such a use of images.

Clearly, in the BBC footage, the insets and the sepia tinting have the further effect of signalling such shots as 'portraits from the Hall of Fame'. By moving into colour whilst within a shot and fading down to tint again within a subsequent shot, the sequence is also able to suggest that most important of Olympic ideas – the continuity of 'greatness' across the sporting past and present. Today's victors (in the final programmes, a shot of Daley Thompson was chosen) have their own future as past champions affirmed in the distinction conferred by the faded brown image. The torch-bearer's movements across the contrasting imagery of the graphics trace Olympian affinities across the broader gap between the Classical and the Modern. A more general point to make about this introductory section as a whole is how well it appears to fit in with the *scheduling* of the coverage. The BBC hoped that many viewers would selectively watch *Olympic Grandstand*'s live output, which started on most evenings at around 11 p.m. It was, then, particularly appropriate to have a relaxing and relatively soft theme tune to open the programmes, rather than a brassy, upbeat number of the type more conventional within sports broadcasting. And the strong emphasis given to the flames in the final graphics sequence is similarly well-suited to the introducing of events which, in Britain, largely happened during the night, beginning well after dark. The effect is nicely predicted by the cover picture of the *Radio Times* for the first week of the Games. It shows a flaming torch being passed from one person's hand to another's against the background of the L.A. stadium arches and the night sky.

Although I've concentrated here on the gateway to the coverage, various elements from it are picked up and combined with other devices of 'celebratory seeing' throughout the programmes. For instance, in the shots of the medals ceremonies, themselves frequently incorporated back into the introductory footage. Here, the use of facial close-ups and superimposition (shots of flags and of faces looking at flags), the music of the anthems and the drawn-out business of hoisting the flags combined to provide the viewer with opportunities for voyeuristic nationalism completely unavailable to the live spectator. During the anthem playing, the very peak of the orchestrated intensity ('now, the moment that gets to us all' – commentator at Lake Casitas), the image which TV sought most strenuously to win for its viewers' delectation seemed to be that of *the bursting through of tears of pride*.

Small wonder, then, that the spell-breaking sight of Daley Thompson cheerfully *whistling* the National Anthem from the podium drew critical comments from the BBC presenter.

The winners of another British 'gold', the rowing team's Coxed Four, behaved far more fittingly for televisation when it was time for them (and us) to be 'got to'. And in the final 'highlights-set-to-music' sequence (a sort of Olympics pop video) screened on the last day, it was their reward to have a very slow panning shot of their tilted faces profiled against the sky given the bleached-out whiteness of ethereal glory. With a shot of the flagstaff superimposed, this was a truly

Chariots style piece of tele-celebration.

The significance of these various examples goes beyond the function which TV's tricks of fragmentation and re-assembly play in 'holding' us as the spectators of its festive and dynamic world of sport. On display here, more obviously than within the less exuberant conventions of news and current affairs, is the medium's proclivity to claim maximum immediacy and raw knowledge ('*see* this *now* and *know*!') in precisely those sequences where it is most closely in collusion with dominant evaluations, stereo-types and assumptions; with the elements of public mythology. TV, we note, may act not only to reproduce these elements but to underpin them with the 'evidence' of its selected visual truths, its 'reportage'. Finally, it's those central (and often politically expedient) myths of 'coverage' which the showbiz inventiveness of sports programming unintentionally helps us to deny.

Colin McArthur

TV Commercials: Moving Statues and Old Movies

'I like the adverts; it's the movies I can't stand.' This famous riposte constitutes, in some respects, a defensible position. A case could be made, though it would not be a very significant critical activity, for the relative merits of television commercials over the programmes that interrupt them. Certainly, in terms of production values, many commercials display flagrantly the fact that they have had ten times as much money spent on them, and the discipline of working within a one to three minute format can have the effect of sharpening narrative skill and honing wit.

Insofar as television commercials have been discussed critically, it has been in terms such as these, apart from the very necessary ideological critique laid on them by, among others, the women's movement. By and large, however, television commercials have been conceived of as 'other' among television's output, as separable from and discussable in terms different from programmes, even within those critical stances which take a 'flow' model of the evening's viewing. Substantial work has been done on, for example, news and current affairs, soap opera, and sit-com television programmes, with regard to their overall shape, the working practices of their personnel, the ideological tendencies of the programmes and their relationship to the institutional framework out of which they come. Such an approach, of course, requires programmes like *News at Ten*, *Panorama*, *Coronation Street* and *It Ain't Half Hot, Mum* to be conceived not as separate, autonomous objects, but to be seen generically as having formal structures and relationships and being subject to transformations connected to events within television and film practice and to the wider society. Analogous work on television commercials would have to begin by pointing, not to the differences between one commercial and another, but to the similarities.

Over the past several months, two motifs have seemed particularly novel, striking and recurrent within television commercials. One of these motifs is the statue which moves. The first commercial to include this was for biscuits, with the statues in a fountain becoming animated in response to the degree of enjoyment experienced by the figures seated by the fountain when eating the biscuits in question.

This was followed by a commercial for a torch battery in which two policemen in Trafalgar Square are struck dumb by the statue of Nelson alighting from its column. This particular realisation of the moving statue motif, related to quite another television phenomenon, was reprised on the cover of *Radio Times*, indicating that cultural practices (in this case the making of television commercials and the design of magazines) do not exist in a vacuum but interact with each other, reworking the same motifs. Several other television commercials deployed the moving statue motif and, by a happy chance, a more recent example included this and the other novel, striking and recurrent impulse of the last few months, the reference to and/or the cutting in of footage from old movies.

Two recent commercials for British Telecom refer to films, one to *Tarzan* and the other to *The Hunchback of Notre Dame*. In the latter, a figure made up like Quasimodo (or, more accurately, as Charles Laughton playing Quasimodo) receives a telephone call from Esmerelda and shares his delight with an animated gargoyle on the roof of Notre Dame cathedral. It is difficult to be certain, but this particular commercial may have used, for the crowd scenes, intercut footage from the thirties' film *The Hunchback of Notre Dame*. If so, this would link it to several such intercuttings in (mainly) television commercials of the last few months. A recent commercial for the Kelly Girl secretarial agency intercuts footage shot in the here-and-now with material from the German silent film *Metropolis*, a film also appropriated in the Queen video promo *Radio GaGa*. However, the most systematic use of earlier films has been in the series of commercials for Holsten lager, in which new footage of Griff Rhys Jones is intercut with footage of Humphrey Bogart, James Cagney, George Raft and John Wayne from movies of the thirties and forties in which they appeared, to make coherent mini-narratives.

What, then, is the meaning of these two recurrences in television commercials? It might be useful at this stage to introduce a concept formulated and used within recent French structuralist and post-structuralist literary theory, the concept of *intertextuality*; crudely, the idea of works of art and discourses feeding off and dissolving into each other. The concept was fashioned to deal with two problems. The first is the widely-held view that the producer of a piece of work (poet, novelist, sculptor or film director) is in some sense wholly the originating source of that work, with the concomitant practice of explaining the work primarily by reference to the personal qualities and background of the artist. The French structuralist and post-structuralist theoretical tradition is concerned with the extent to which the institutions of language and literature and their specific forms (the realist novel, the fantastic, etc.) predate their deployment by particular artists who, therefore, can no more be said to 'invent' their works than the speaker of a particular language can be said to invent that language. Challengingly, it has been asserted that texts produce authors rather than authors texts.

The second problem the concept of *intertextuality* was fashioned to deal with is the widely-held predisposition to assume that the most pertinent relationships a work has are with the 'real' world to which it refers, a predisposition particularly deeply grounded with regard to photographic practices such as cinema and television. *Intertextuality*, on the contrary, asserts that a more pertinent relationship exists between a particular work and the other works in the system or genre (e.g., the picaresque novel, the *film noir*, the television soap opera) to which it belongs. Indeed, one of the suggestions associated with *intertextuality* is that a reader's ability to understand a particular form is dependent upon her exposure to previous examples of it, so that, for example, a particular kind of music above the opening credits and an opening image of a dark, rain-soaked street will set in train a range of expectations in the viewer as to what will follow (the expectations will partially have been aroused by the way the film has been publicised).

Clearly the lager commercials referred to above are *intertexts* in a very fundamental way: they cut together footage of different decades. However, the commercials with the moving statue motif are also *intertexts* in the sense that they 'quote' from earlier commercials (and, as will be suggested, film). The deployment of a concept such as *intertextuality* over the terrain of television commercials (a process which would, doubtless, cause their makers to raise their eyebrows) yields precisely the same benefits as its deployment on more 'serious' forms. That is to say, it points to the fact that they are not simply separate and autonomous objects spinning out of the talent and imagination of their makers but that, perhaps more pertinently, they exist in relationship with each other, as phenomena shaped within shared cultural determinants.

What some of these determinants are might be speculated upon quite concretely with regard to the moving statue and old movies motifs. About 18 months ago the film *The Draughtsman's Contract* opened in London to considerable critical acclaim from the 'heavy' press and had a long run in a London 'art house'. Among its motifs (formally inventive or flashy, according to one's view of what constitutes excellence in the cinema) was a statue which not only moved but urinated. Almost contemporaneous with this was the opening of the American movie *Dead Men Don't Wear Plaid*, a 'send-up' of the American crime movie which intercut footage from earlier movies in the same genre into its narrative. Both films achieved a kind of 'cult' status, being appropriated by the camp sensibility, by which is meant a sensibility which appropriates art in a hermetically sealed kind of way, to produce meanings and pleasures which have no point of purchase on the wider social and political life of the society. Speculatively, the camp sensibility would seem to be very prevalent among the personnel and institutions which make up the world of television commercials. It is a sensibility uniquely well-fashioned for the job is it required to do and the interests it, for the most part, serves.

Albert Hunt

'She laughed at me with my own teeth': Tommy Cooper — Television Anti-Hero

A few days after comedian Tommy Cooper died, fellow-comedian Ernie Wise, told a story about him on television. Tommy Cooper, said Ernie Wise, had gone into a restaurant and ordered a cup of hot coffee. The coffee, he had insisted, must be hot and steaming. So the waiter had brought him a cup of hot, steaming coffee.

Tommy Cooper had held the cup of coffee in his hand and had begun, as Ernie Wise put it, to talk to 'Eric and I'. By the time he got round to tasting the coffee, it had gone cool. 'But I asked you to bring me *hot* coffee,' he expostulated to the waiter. 'That,' said Ernie Wise, 'was Tommy Cooper.'

The story, as Ernie Wise told it, wasn't particularly funny. But if you imagine it as it might have been performed by Tommy Cooper himself, on-stage, you're taken into another dimension.

'For my next trick, I'll need a cup of steaming hot coffee.' A cup of steaming hot coffee is put into Tommy Cooper's hands. 'Now this coffee,' he announces in a loud, strangulated voice – then looks round in bewilderment. 'Why am I shouting?' He puts the coffee down. 'Now I'd like someone at random in the audience to think of a card. Mr. Random? No, don't tell me the card you've thought of.' He places a pack of cards in front of a mechanical duck and, to make it more difficult, he blindfolds the duck. The duck picks out a card. 'Now, what was your card?' he asks the man in the audience, and when the man tells him, he says, 'You're right,' and throws the card away without showing it. He picks up the cup of coffee, almost puts it to his lips, then says, 'I'd like to tell you a quick joke.' He pauses – the pause wins him a laugh. 'I've forgotten it,' he says, then goes into a long, rambling story about a monkey, a lion and a laughing hyena. 'And now I'd like to sing for you.' Finally, he picks up the cup, tastes the coffee and spits it out. 'I said the coffee had to be steaming hot!' Now that *was* Tommy Cooper.

To Tommy Cooper, the everyday world was a place in which things happen that defy belief. Hot coffee goes cool, simply because you don't drink it – how can such things be? Water tastes of nothing – 'It'll never sell,' he comments as he takes a gulp while setting up an immensely complicated trick involving glasses of water and fresh eggs. When you pass your hand through a flame, you get burnt! Tommy Cooper revealed this unbelievable world to us in the commonplace box that sits in the corner of every living room.

Tommy Cooper, like Morecambe and Wise, came out of the world of music-hall and variety. But he belonged to television. Because it was in the ordered, neatly packaged world of television that the anarchic nature of Tommy Cooper's world was most fully displayed.

The world of television is essentially small and cosy. There is constant *talk* of calamity. Bombs explode in Belfast (we see pictures of the blaze); children die in Africa, villagers are shot in El Salvador, a naval officer in Polaris shows us the key he'll use to end the world. But it's all as unreal as *Starsky and Hutch* or *Dallas*. The reality is Sue Lawley in the safety of her studio.

The world of Tommy Cooper is much more dangerous. He fills four glasses with water, then he shows the audience an egg-box full of eggs, six of them. 'Now, if someone would choose an egg at random. Mr. Random? Choose any egg. This one? You're sure you don't want that one?' He breaks the egg into the water jug to prove the eggs are real.

Then he puts a tray on top of the four glasses of water, and on the tray he balances four upright tubes, and on the tubes he balances four eggs. He explains that when he hits the tray with the side of his hand – 'Like that. Or I might hit it like that,' demonstrating a side-swipe – the four eggs are supposed to drop into the four glasses of water: 'And I'm wondering why it never works.' He stands contemplating the eggs.

He looks thoughtfully at the audience. There are some people, he explains, who, if it doesn't work, are in the direct line of fire. But they shouldn't worry. 'If an egg flies towards you, catch it like that,' – he cups his hands gently together. 'Not like that.' He claps his big hands sharply together, then pretends to wipe egg off the front of his jacket. The eggs stay balanced on the tubes while he wanders off to do another trick.

The audience, of course, has no real worries. Studio audiences don't expect to get eggs thrown at them in respectable, mainstream shows. And the world of television lives on confirming expectations.

Characters on television, from Hilda Ogden to Margaret Thatcher, behave in the way we expect them to behave. Hilda Ogden will always gossip; Margaret Thatcher will always demonstrate her voice-trained sincerity. Moderates will talk like moderates; extremists will rant like extremists. Mass pickets will always be violent; the Russians will always be unreasonable. The voice that brings you the unbiased news will always be the voice of respectable, southern middle-class England (make Hilda Ogden a newsreader and the news loses its credibility and is revealed as the nation's gossip).

Tommy Cooper, of course, also fulfils expectations – up to a point. We know that he will appear in his red fez. We expect him to make the characteristic gesture with his arms – 'Not like that, like that.' And we know he'll do magic that goes wrong. But the *way* it goes wrong is constantly surprising. He *plays* with our expectations.

He borrows a white handkerchief from a very smartly-dressed middle-aged man in the audience: 'Mr. Random?' He holds the handkerchief in his left fist in such a way that the middle of the handkerchief is fluffed out on top. He looks at the handkerchief, looks up and gives the familiar laugh – 'Huh, huh.'

He takes his cigarette lighter in his right hand and swiftly sets fire to the middle of the handkerchief. So he's doing the trick where he sets fire to something and then shows the audience it hasn't been burned? Very dramatically, he holds out his right hand. So he's going to do the old circus trick of passing a hand through a flame without being hurt? He passes his hand through the flame and cries out in pain – he sucks his burnt fingers. Triumphantly, he opens the white handkerchief and holds it up to the audience. There's a big, jagged burnt hole in the middle of the handkerchief. 'Never mind,' he says to the man in the audience, 'I'll give you mine,' – and we suddenly notice the white handkerchief in his own breast pocket. He takes out his handkerchief and holds it up to the audience. There's a big, jagged burnt hole in the middle... To paraphrase Groucho Marx, fire may look as if it burns, and feel as if it burns, but don't let that fool you – it really does burn.

Tommy Cooper works hard at making things appear to go wrong – whereas the world of television works hard at making things appear to go right. Television tries to stick together carefully selected fragments of reality in such a way that, as Eric Morecambe would have said, 'You can't see the join.' Whether it's bringing you highlights of the match of the day, or an edited version of the Trades' Union Congress, television tries to make you believe that you're seeing the flow of events as they occurred. The mechanics of the trade are carefully hidden.

Tommy Cooper gleefully displays the mechanics of his trade. He places an empty vase on a stand. 'I am now going to make flowers appear in this varse or vayse,' he announces. He drapes a cloth over the vase, utters words of magic and then whips the cloth triumphantly away. No flowers have appeared. Carefully, he places the cloth back over the vase and utters the words of magic again. He whips the cloth away – still no flowers have appeared.

He removes the vase from the stand with his right hand, and with his left hand, in full view of the audience, he adjusts a spring mechanism on the stand. He is on the point of replacing the vase on the stand when flowers leap out of the stand and into his left hand. He stuffs the flowers into the vase. And asks for applause.

No area of the world of television tries harder to hide the mechanics and to get things right than the area of drama. Naturalism – the pretence that what we're seeing is a representation of 'real life' – rules virtually unchallenged in television drama. The Ken Loach school of social realism, usually seen as Britain's most-admired contribution to world TV drama, measures its own success by the extent to which it is realer than thou. And the Cedric Messina school of Shakespearian production even tries to make Shakespeare naturalistic, with cameras wandering over halls and battlements and the blank verse an embarrassment to be hidden.

Tommy Cooper has his own approach to Shakespeare. He appears on an obvious Victorian-style stage, dressed as a ham actor, and makes all the extravagant ham gestures. He declaims:

> 'To be or not to be, that is the question.
> Whether 'tis nobler in the mind to suffer
> The slings and arrows of outrageous fortune. . . .'

He breaks off and we see him in close-up. 'I had a bit of bad luck myself yesterday,' he says. 'Got nicked for parking. I said to the traffic warden, 'But I'm parked in a cul-de-sac.' He said, 'I don't care what kind of a car you're parked in. . . .'

> 'Or to take arms against a sea of troubles. . . .'

'I usually travel by sea. . . .'

He takes liberties, too, with an area of British drama that's even more sacred that Shakespeare – the Second World War prison camp epic. He enters wearing a uniform that's British khaki down the right side and SS black down the left. We are, he explains, in a prison camp in the Rhineland in 1941, and a British officer is being interrogated. On the right side of his upper lip, he sticks an enormous false handle-bar moustache. In his left eye he puts a monocle.

When the British officer is speaking, Tommy Cooper places himself in right profile, so that only the khaki uniform and the false moustache can be seen. But when he speaks for the SS interrogator, he makes no such attempt to be convincing: he's nearly face on to the camera, and he struggles constantly with the monocle, which keeps falling out. The SS interrogator points to the letters SS on his sleeve: 'You know what these letters stand for?' Sssssssss . . . Sssssssilence!' The monocle drops out – he struggles to put it back in. 'These letters stand for the dreaded organisation that these letters stand for.' 'The

Sea Scouts?' 'Yes. The dreaded Sea Scouts.' The monocle falls out. The interrogator says he's going to shoot the British officer and asks him if he has one last request. 'Could I have a cigarette?' The interrogator struggles desperately and long with his monocle. Finally, he has it fixed. 'Nein!' he shrieks. 'But I only want one' – this from the British officer very quickly. The interrogator struggles again for a long time with his monocle. Once again he gets it fixed. 'But I only want one,' says the interrogator in the British officer's accent. The monocle falls. Tommy Cooper looks at the camera. 'I don't know where I am,' he says.

During the long, long meander around tricks and jokes which he takes after he's set up the eggs on the four upright tubes on the tray on the four glasses of water, Tommy Cooper says, 'I'll tell you what I'll do. I'd like to sing for you now if I may.' He begins to sing, 'As time goes by':

> 'Moonlight and love songs usually out of date,
> Hearts full of passion, jealousy and hate,
> Woman needs man, and man must have his mate. . . .'

Then he breaks off, and delivers a sentimental monologue, with the piano tinkling softly in the background: 'Yes, I shall never forget the first time I met her. She was sitting on top of Waterloo Bridge, dangling her feet in the water. . . . She had wavy hair all down her back. Not on her head, all down her back. And she had very unusual lips, both on top. And she had protruding teeth, right through her upper lip. And I said to her, "I'll take you to a dentist." So I took her to a dentist and I got her the best set of teeth that money could buy. And then she left me – just like that.' He pauses and makes the familiar gesture with his arms – 'Not like that – like that.' Then he goes back into his monologue. 'And finally, when I saw her again' – the look of disbelief comes into his face – 'she laughed at me. *With my own teeth.*'

Tommy Cooper spent much of his life laughing at the solemn orthodoxies of television with its own teeth. I don't suppose, when he made clocks disappear and re-appear in the most surprising places, or said, in passing, 'I had a cigarette lighter that wouldn't go out,' that he ever consciously thought of himself as subverting the ordered world. But his art was – is – in that popular English tradition that the playwright John Arden once described as being 'quite astonishingly hostile to good. . . . order.' And in a television industry that was set up by authority, is controlled by authority, and invariably presents a balanced picture on the side of authority, his anarchic spirit was very welcome.

He didn't, incidentally, send the fresh eggs flying towards the audience. He said, 'If I get just one egg in a glass it'll be all right, won't it?' And, in fact, he got two eggs in. And put the other two in by hand. And accepted the applause he'd honestly earned.

David Lusted

The Glut of the Personality

Jimmy Saville, Tracey Ullman, Denis Waterman, Lenny Henry, Clive James, Jan Leeming.... Personalities are central to the institution of television. A stock of recognised names acts as an assurance that audiences will return again (and again) to their role as viewers, perpetuating – via advertising or licence revenue – the flow of cash to maintain the institution. There is an economic imperative, then, to television's construction and maintenance of personalities.

The assurance is like an informal contract between production company and audience. Yet, in the same way that promises can be broken, the assurance is no guarantee. It is less a contract than a mythology, for the most part sustained in the face of regular and consistent contrary evidences. The popularity of any personality can rise and fall repetitively. (Yesterday's has-been may be today's discovery and ripe for anonymity tomorrow. Ask Frankies Vaughan and Howerd.) And audiences have been known to refuse the offer of many a personality in particular programmes or series. Nonetheless, as a *system*, like cinema's star system, the mythology has material effects: the production of more personalities in the relentless search for high viewing figures.

The mythology is sustained, of course, by cultural myths beyond television. The cult of the personality is a product of *the myth of the individual*. According to this myth, history is made by extraordinary men (and a few women), irrespective of social movements. The myth has two inflections. One stresses individual achievement through personal effort and competition, and particularly serves the interests of capital. The other is the folk myth (the Cinderella story or the Log-Cabin-to-White-House story) in which the individual succeeds through nature or fate, rather than effort, position or circumstance. The first inflection foregrounds labour, the second denies it and offers genius in its place. The myth of individualism, like all myths, is contradictory.

Nowhere is contradiction more apparent than in television, where the constant need to top up the stock produces a veritable *glut* of personalities, a process which, once acknowledged, exposes the myth of the *rare* individual.

'I knew her for a long, long time. She was a marvellous woman, a one-off, like Tommy Cooper.'

*Eric Morecambe, on the death of Diana Dors (*Daily Mail, *5/5/1984)*

Television's personality system dominantly reproduces myths of individualism, then. Yet this statement takes no account of the pleasures sought from or delivered by the system, nor does it allow for different, especially *social*, meanings to appear. If the individualist mythology is contradictory so, too, may be the personality system. Within those contradictions the social groups who make up factions of television's audiences may also find alternative recognitions, affirmations and identifications that are even oppositional to the dominant tendencies of television's personality system.

The coincidence of the deaths of Tommy Cooper (15/4/84), Diana Dors (4/5/84) and Eric Morecambe (27/6/84) offers a convenient (if sad) pretext for a case study to explore these possibilities. Let us see how certain TV personalities may provide pleasures for certain factions of audiences through *social* meanings in opposition to both the personality system and the myth of individualism.

First, recall that the particular biographies of the three reach before and beyond the television institution. They are not just *television* personalities. Cooper and Morecambe were both comedy stars of the variety circuit (music-halls, cabaret, clubs, etc.) before and during their television celebrity. Dors was a film-star of the sub-species 'sex symbol' and an actress respected for 'difficult' roles (as, for instance, 'Ruth Ellis' in *Yield to the Night*). To this we must add their appearance in television forms that exceeded their origins. Cooper and Morecambe starred in their own light entertainment variety shows on television, as well as guesting (Cooper much more than Morecambe) on the shows of other stars. Dors acted in innumerable fictions, from drama to situation comedy. But also they all appeared in chat shows, game shows, magazines. . . . Morecambe, for instance, appeared as himself in an episode of the crime-series *The Sweeney* and, through his connections with Luton Football Club, was frequently sought for interviews on sports programmes. Cooper was as frequent a speaker at televised showbiz functions and a favourite of filmed comedy shorts made by another comic, Eric Sykes. Dors appeared in variety shows as a singer and in sketches. She hosted her own chat show for a period and ran a slimming feature for breakfast television shortly before her death. All three, then, whilst identifiable as specialists, were also *icons of intertextuality*. More than personalities, they were television stars, embodying a rich repertoire of reference in popular cultural memory. The point to stress here is that through their many and varied appearances, their names connected with many factions of audiences, for each of which the meaning of any personality will vary.

What, then, becomes an issue is isolating their *potential* for social meaning in one or many of the types of appearance for particular factions of audience. And, if we are interested in ascribing affirmations, recognitions and identifications they offer to the broadest working-class (but raced, aged and gendered) audiences, it is the *particularities* of the potential meanings they offer those audiences that require attention. My argument will be that each of these personalities connect a specific range of affirmations, recognitions and identifications to specific audience formations, whilst remaining broad and/or complex enough to aggregate majority audiences.

Much of the pleasure of forms of television's light entertainment comes not only from recognising the skills of personalities (from the physical dexterity of the juggler or magician to the verbal constructions of the raconteur) but also the *risks* at stake. Local failure is always potential and sometimes actual, from the dropped Indian club or transparent illusion to the verbal *faux-pas*. Indeed, Tommy Cooper's comic magician and Eric Morecambe's comic dupe acknowledge and incorporate the pleasure of the risk into their performance personas. These personas admit what the personality system recognises but attempts to efface – the risks of performance. Moreover, the Cooper and Morecambe personalities recognise that audience complicity is central to such an exposure; it becomes a point of negotiation, pleasurable in itself, between personality and audience. For much of light entertainment the recognition is suppressed in the interests of success and the confirmation of talented individuals. In musical variety, for instance, only comedian Les Dawson's off-key piano plays with discord and there is no tradition of *singing* off-key, even in fun. Part of the pleasure of games shows, quizzes and 'talent' contests, for instance, is precisely that they *foreground* the risk of failure; their extraordinary popularity should be no surprise.

The supreme risk, however, is of failure to maintain not just an individual performance but the faith in success and talent underpinning showbiz itself. The risk operates as a neurosis around light entertainment, comparable to that of the myth of individual skill and effort as a guarantor of economic achievement and social status which is at odds with all working-class experience and some working-class consciousness. Diana Dors, pre-eminently, was a personality who declared that risk and threatened that myth in the active manipulation of her own complex persona.

In sum, then, the myths of success and talent routinely risk pleasurable exposure within the *form* of light entertainment, yet the pleasures and meaning of certain personalities derive from their regular de-mystification of that process.

'There have been times that I have known disappointment, even despair. The public never realised because I was laughing on the outside while crying on the inside. Very dangerous – you could easily drown.'

Tommy Cooper, Daily Star *(11/11/82)*

There is a simple sense in which all three personalities shared a 'common touch', an expression of collusion with the materiality of working-class life. Unlike personalities such as, say, Michael Parkinson, David Frost or Selina Scott – who represent the cultures of manual and/or domestic labour at one remove, as it were – Cooper, Morecambe and Dors represent a direct and experiential identification with the materiality of working-classness; pub culture over wine bar, soccer over cricket, nappies over nannies. Crudely, it is a matter of class cultural embodiment. Yet there is a more complex sense in which these three personalities can be understood as *social* stars and it exists in their critical distance from the central meanings and functions of the personality system.

All television personalities in non-fiction forms affect connections with their audiences. Through forms of direct address that characteristically punctuate variety (semi-confessionally), chat shows and magazines (familiarly) and news programmes (more formally) alike, appeals to commonality and consensus are supreme. The wit of Cooper, Morecambe and Dors serves as comment on that operation. Cooper employed surreal inanities ('I used to collect dust but I gave it up,' and 'I take my drinks neat – but sometimes I let my shirt tail hang out a bit'); Morecambe parodied, through asides like 'This boy's a fool!' and in a range of exchanges to camera, especially when feigning ignorance of guest stars in his shows with Ernie Wise; Dors could also use a comic mode but, more often, used caustic put-downs on personalities around her whose bonhomie grew excessive ('Calm down, there's a good boy'). These verbal (combined with gestural) devices mark off a distance from the rhetoric of personality, individuating our three personalities as *commentators* upon as well as *collaborators* in the system. These counter-rhetorical devices, colluding with the audience at the expense of the personality system, construct a more social connection to audiences familiar with and attracted by that system.

'For most people life is a bloody awful grind. They do jobs they hate – if they are lucky enough to have a job. So when someone comes along who makes them forget their troubles, it's a relief for them.'

Tommy Cooper, Daily Star, *16/4/84*

All three personalities embody certain characteristics of working-class experience in their performances and, arousingly, in their particular manipulations of the formal strategies and institutional practices of television. In their embodiment of working-class experience, they recognise a sense of 'working-classness' as special and discrete from other class experience. In their manipulation of television they represent a separation from controlling definitions of convention and normality. In the combination of embodiment and manipulation, they affirm the subordinated but, crucially, unbowed and resilient properties of working-class experience.

There is another sense in which the three personalities affirm qualities of class resilience, Cooper most resonantly. Cooper's obsessive failure at effecting magic tricks corresponds symbolically to the systematic lack of fit between investment in and rewards of labour. The deployment of humour – in a series of unconnected, surprising and excessive jokes delivered in a bemused, self-deprecating manner – connects precisely with the wit characteristic of groups in manual and domestic labour, effectively a stoical commentary on the absurdity of their class conditions, 'working your end away' to minimal material effect. This quality has its biographical equivalent in Cooper's long history of heart, liver and chest complaints which progressively slurred his speech and slowed his actions. Made visible to his audiences by surrounding publicity but never self-promoted or acknowledged in performance, this biographical recognition adds to that sense of stoicism in the face of personal adversity. Similarly, Morecambe's heart disease and Dors' thyroid complaint (responsible for her size) and, later, cancer, were tragic components of their personal biographies but also recognised sub-texts of their personas. Struggling against debility, the shared knowledge of their frail mortality acts as a recognised, but unspoken, bond of recognition between personality and audience. Undoubtedly, recognition of mortality is classless, but *labouring* through that knowledge has an added frisson for working-class consciousness, in which death through industrial disease and premature ageing has acute meaning. In many ways, the *life-style* of showbiz, too, its display of excessive high-living, is a symbolic equivalent to the 'live now, pay later' component of working-class culture so deprecated by moralists of the left and centre alike. For the disadvantaged sections of a capitalist economy, at the bottom of the social order, the choice between convention and compliance or refusal and pleasure is not easy. Punishment is the return on both choices but at least, with the latter, there is some fun on the way. Cooper and Dors, especially, can be seen – like Judy Garland and Sid Vicious before them – as exponents of that choice but also as its tragic victims. The tragedy of Cooper and Dors, however, has a vivid connection to working-class consciousness. In that context, a buoyant resilience to the physical punishment rendered by the catch-22 of 'the system' has a particular currency.

Recognitions of expressions and forms of resilience are crucial to connecting the popularity of these personalities with their audiences and are not to be denied an importance in sustaining the routine survival tactics of day-to-day oppression.

Nonetheless, resilience alone carries the risk of affirming survival at the expense of transformation. The individualism of these personalities would amount to little more than confirmation of class oppression if it did not also encourage forms of resistance through symbolic calls for social change, models of possibilities and outcomes, and strategies to effect them. Morecambe's claim to attention here is specific and conscious. It resides in a particular camera style and address to camera that developed around his manipulation of the stereotype comic fool. The stereotype conventionally takes one of two forms – either the overbearing boor (e.g., Les Dawson, Bruce Forsyth and, earlier, Bob Hope – and earliest, Punchinello) or the hapless pre-adolescent (e.g., Michael Crawford's Frank Spencer, Frank Crompton and, earlier, Jerry Lewis – and, earliest, Harlequin). Like only W. C. Fields before him – and unique in a double act – Morecambe combines these alternatives, but in a particular way. The Morecambe persona is at once arrogantly self-confident, freely insulting, hyper-active *and* easily (if temporarily) defused, consistently slighted, constantly ignored. Forms of attention-seeking such as these are conventionally dismissed as juvenile or lunatic, especially in the social world where deviant characteristics are regularly ascribed to politically-oppositional activity in conflict with the status quo. In particular, strikes, demonstrations and picketing can be labelled 'silly' or 'childlike' in order to depoliticise their purpose, deny them rationality and change (consciousness of) their effect. The sophistication of Morecambe's comic persona and the formal differences in its comic context disavows such epithets and puts the lie (for those in the audience socially positioned to recognise it) to similar terms of denunciation in the social world. Instead, Morecambe affirms the appropriateness of forms of opposition and ascribes status to them.

In particular, the formal devices employed by Morecambe – the regular exchange of looks with the audience aside from the sketch or fiction those around him inhabit, his reactions to their attempts to disturb his disruption – affirm a range of *tactical* strategies. They affirm oppositional practices in the face of dominant assurances that they are not necessary; they resist incorporation and demand recognition as right; they are resilient but also resist attempts at modification. In sum, they symbolically affirm subordinated class struggle and evidence not only tactics to survive but strategies to resist.

These particular recognitions connect most clearly with existing forms of organised political opposition, especially within the labour movement, and it is to factions of audiences drawn from such groups that the Morecambe persona and situations offer particular confirmations. For other factions, too, the persona may initiate recognitions and/or inform a developing politicised consciousness.

Where Morecambe *used* the conventions of music-hall and television's direct address, Cooper subverted them. Rehearsals for his shows were notoriously chaotic; refusing scripts, repeatedly missing chalk marks, inserting new routines and one-liners. The shambles of rehearsals were evident to audiences of his performances. A nightmare for programme directors and camera operators, Cooper's performances meant that the camera was invariably in the wrong position at the wrong time. Effectively, gags were lost as punchlines were delivered off-frame, the climaxes of routines were witnessed by a mis-framed camera and longueurs occurred wherein no one seemed sure of intentions. Cooper, in sum, was anarchy to the television institution. The same unpredictability characterised his many 'personal' appearances. A speech for a televised celebrity function comprised breathless nothings as he feigned loss of speech, then a faulty microphone; witness to another's *This Is Your Life*, he affected ignorance of the celebrity he was called to celebrate: 'Never heard of him,' he offered to the teeth-gritting smile of Eamonn Andrews.

Cooper's inability to perform according to any rules affirms a sense of opposition. Yet his iconoclasm is always tempered by control and calm. The form of disruption he represents is an affirmation of a more militant strand of working-class resistance, less regulated, more spontaneous, yet still political. Cooper's logic of no logic is a disruptive tactic, not just in labour politics but also in domestic and other areas of social life.

Finally, Diana Dors. Dors worked centrally, neither on the conventions or forms of television, but transparently on its nature as institution. Publicity-conscious from the earliest days of her cinema career, Dors manipulated television's promotional machinery. In a career strewn with personal scandal and professional disputes with managements (in the best showbiz tradition) the distinction between a chaotic lifestyle and self-promotion was rarely clear. Yet, through this, developed a highly reflexive use of the Dors persona.

Established initially as a sex-symbol, she refused the connotations of dumb sexuality. Always self-conscious of the type, she wasted few chances to expose – through exaggerated gestures of female sexuality and a sneering disdain for on-screen predatory males (no-one curled a lip like Dors) – its construction in male voyeurism. Yet, skilfully, the licence of her own sexuality was not lost in the process and the sense of a woman in control, manipulating within the constraints, was paramount. As she aged, she pushed at the connotations of a variant type known as 'the good time girl', retaining its characteristic self-regulating search for pleasure, but denying its characterisation as sin, and crossing the type with another in its celebration of activity in motherhood. Her conversation in chat shows was peppered with risqué tales, putting the life into family life, breaking the conventional models of femininity and domesticity. Her challenge to these conventions made her a risk to the institution, hence the short-term irregularity of her appearances, but this merely served to imbue her appearances with critical resonances. Dors offered a challenging model in an antagonistic relation to the meaning of roles customarily allocated to (especially working-class) women and it is likely that the model would connect with the experience and aspirations of that gendered audience. The pleasure she displayed in female company, especially other sexually-available mothers like Marti Caine; the negotiated control she exercised over male groups, especially in fictions like *Queenie's Castle*; the assertiveness at odds with her torch songs; all these offered tactical strategies for changing male-centred discourses about woman's role in heterosexual partnerships and family relations.

Dors disturbed a range of female roles on television. In so doing, she offered connections with women of all ages in a comparable variety of social roles, recognising their experience, demonstrating possibilities for change within that experience and offering models of alternative possibilities. It's also worth asserting – not least to explain the pleasures for *men* in her performances – that Dors also holds out pleasures in these changes for men troubled by conventional models of male-regulated heterosexual relationships and the unattainable (and undesired) ideals of masculinity those models inscribe.

Finally, whatever the merits or limitations of this particular case-study, I hope it indicates a requirement of cultural criticism to explore structures and strategies of opposition *within* the mythologies of television, especially in the relation of television to its audiences. The requirement is not least in order to avoid breaking faith, not only with the interests of the many factions of the working-class who comprise television's audiences, but also with the pleasures and politically-oppositional meanings many in those audiences derive from television. This is an area of famine in cultural criticism which would benefit from a sudden glut.

Bibliography

Rick Altman (ed). *Genre: The Musical* (Routledge, 1981).

Richard Dyer, *Stars*, BFI 1979. 'Entertainment & Utopia', *Movie* no. 24, Spring, 1977, pp. 2–13, reprinted in Altman (1981). *Light Entertainment*, TV Monograph no. 2, BFI, 1973.

John Ellis, 'Star/Industry/Image', *Star Signs*, BFI, 1981. 'Made in Ealing', *Screen*, Spring, 1975, vol. 16, no. 1 (especially pages 113–118).

Jeff Nuttall, *King Twist: A Biography of Frank Randle*, Routledge, 1978.

With thanks to Jim Cook for supportive criticism.

Charlotte Brunsdon

Writing about Soap Opera

Soap operas, such as *Crossroads*, *Coronation Street* and *Brookside* do not just exist in the hour or so of broadcast television a week that each is allotted. The central fiction of the genre, that the communities represented exist outside the box, as well as on it – the idea that the Grants, or Ken and Deidre, or Jill and Adam could watch the news, just like us – is supported and sustained across a range of media material. Newspaper articles, novels, souvenir programmes, *TV Times* promotions, even cookery books, function to support the simultaneous co-existence of them and us.[1] It is possible to wear the same clothes, use the same decor, follow the same recipes, and even pore over the same holiday snaps as the people in the Street, the Close and the Motel. It is even possible to buy *Ambridge, An English Village through the Ages*, the book that Jennifer Aldridge and John Tregorran researched and wrote together while listeners nationwide followed their growing pleasure in each other's company.[2]

The promotional material produced by the television companies and associated bodies, and the spin-off material produced under licence from the television company all work to sustain the reality of the fiction. Much of this material strives quite specifically to implicate the viewer/reader in this suspension of disbelief.[3] The *TV Times*, for example, at moments of soapy ritual like weddings, produces 'snaps' of past weddings and vanished characters. The fan is exhorted to test memory, to remember the televisual past in the same way as we remember our own pasts. That same moment of recognition, 'Oh, look, there's X'/'Do you remember . . .?' followed by the assertion of the naturalness of 'now' – 'Look at that dress/hat/hairdo'. The soap opera world and our world are brought together in this blurring of private and public repertoires.

These are, however, not the only discourses which construct and comment on the soap opera world. 'True stories', usually by cast and ex-cast, and usually in the popular Sundays or weeklies, promise to take the lid off the fiction. Autobiographies by people like Pat Phoenix and Noele Gordon offer glimpses of the relation between personality and character. You can go and see the Archers at agricultural shows. Noele Gordon writes about cancer as *Woman* of the week, 'Dammit, I haven't got time to die' (26/5/84). Some of this material can be thought of as 'soap opera as news'. Exposés are certainly national news. But so are illness, death, legal prosecution, accidents, marriage and divorce of the actors and actresses. Often, these stories of 'real life' run as a kind of sub-text, or parallel soap to the one we watch on television. This sub-text is not kept separate when watching. The knowledge you have about particular characters 'in real life' feeds into and inflects the pleasure of soap watching.

It has been argued that soap operas make their viewers carry on watching because they want to know what will happen next. For the soap fan, one of the moments of pleasure is when you can say 'Oh, I *knew* that was going to happen.' But this is not quite the same feeling as the attendant fascination of *how* it is going to happen. At the moment, I don't really think that Sheila Grant is going to have the baby that she is pregnant with. My reasons are partly generic – I know that a very high proportion of soap opera pregnancies come to little more than a few months' story. They are partly what I experience as 'intuitive' – she is in her forties, she has already got three children, the house isn't big enough. Partly cynical – she's the only character of child-bearing age on the Close who wouldn't have an abortion (Heather, Karen, Michelle (?)) or hasn't already got young children (Marie), so she's the only one that pregnancy will be a big issue for. If I'm right, what I don't know is how she is not going to have it. So my pleasure (rather unpleasantly, in this case) is in how my prediction comes true.

Brilliantly, at this point, *Brookside* has combined Edna Cross's predisposition to a bet with Marie's second sight to allow the viewer to have her predictions explicitly debated on screen. Edna and Marie had a bet about whether Alan and Samantha would finally get married. We all wondered. But as soap opera is news, both in the doings of characters and actors/actresses, and it was 'known' that Dicken Ashworth, who plays Alan, was leaving, the viewer had to juggle another sort of knowledge in the attempt to get the prediction right. Will it be easier for him to be written out if he does or doesn't get married?

So soap opera as news can increase the pleasure of the hermaneutic speculation, as it increases the constraints in play. The viewer has to juggle all the different sorts of knowledge to get it right. With this much practice from television entertainment – and entertainment that is widely regarded as requiring little effort on the part of its addicted viewers – small wonder that we reproduce some of the dominant ideological paradigms in our own lives. Of course, extra-textual determination can become excessive, as has happened in the last eighteen months with *Coronation Street*, where possibility has no dynamism, and the programme keeps having to come up with solutions to one loss after another.

It is not only as news or plot speculation that soap opera features in newspapers. All newspapers have some form of television criticism, and soap opera makes episodic appearances in these columns.

Television criticism in newspapers does not generally directly address soap operas. The regular exception here is Nancy Banks-Smith of *The Guardian*, who not only watches soaps but has a very sharp eye for the use of the soap register in 'life', i.e., other programmes such as The News. The metaphorical value of J. R. Ewing and Alexis Carrington has extended beyond the Entertainments page of most newspapers for some time. However, in the main, soap opera functions, within writing about other programmes, as a symbol of the truly awful. Thus, in a discussion of American television, Rod Allen, writing in *The Listener* (8/7/76), observes that these programmes 'would make *Crossroads* look like Oscar Wilde by comparison.' Reference to *Crossroads* in particular, functions as an abbreviated way of invoking bad scripts, bad acting, cheap sets, poor timing – and *stupid* fans. Thus Sue Arnold, in *The Observer* (8/5/83), discussing the travails of finding a nanny, can say:

'I have had 16-year-olds straight from school with basic common sense whom I would trust implicitly to cross the King's Road with a pram and three ancillary children, and girls with 10 years of experience who would still be watching *Crossroads* when the house burned down.'

As all soaps attract large audiences, and *Crossroads*, for example, in its heyday, was usually watched by about thirteen million people, there is a lurking problem about the nature of television criticism here. There is an uneasy relationship between institutionalized television criticism and popular taste and audience. What is the role of television criticism which can neither explain the popularity of a programme like *Crossroads* nor, indeed, even take this popularity seriously? The repressed question of television criticism can be traced: 'Who is this critic speaking for and to?' Occasionally critics directly address this issue:

To criticize *Crossroads* (ATV) is to criticize sliced white bread, or football or keg beer – you are made to feel it's a class snobbism, you're trying to show yourself superior to what the ordinary people enjoy. Unfortunately, the ordinary people are wrong, and the critic is right and *Crossroads* is bad, slack, inept and untruthful, even within its own miserable limits.

(No author credit) Sunday Telegraph, 6 April, 1975)

This explicitly 'classed' notion of the critic as specialist judge and arbiter of taste is the opposite to the position argued in one of the more substantial defences of soap opera, Dorothy Hobson's book on *Crossroads.*[4] Hobson upbraids television critics for employing critical criteria derived from high art in the evaluation of a popular form such as soap opera, and appears to argue that popularity itself should be a central evaluative criterion. Most usefully, she shows that the audience for *Crossroads* is mainly female and often elderly. Here we begin to see that it is not only issues of class, but also gender and age status of the audience which may inflect critical judgement.

Most critics, however, choose to avoid the question of 'tendency', explicit or otherwise, in critical judgement. There are two main strategies used here, to bridge that gap between critic and audience. The first, which has a long history in relation to popular art forms, and was, for example, used in relation to the novel, is what we could now call the addiction strategy.

The critic and the reader can together perceive the soap opera fan as acting without desire:

'These were the ones with the worst symptoms of withdrawal pains. For them this four times a week shot of soap opera had become as habit forming as a drug'
  (written of Crossroads fans during the 1979 ITV strike, Hilary Kingsley)
  *(*Sunday People, *28/10/79)*

People who become addicted to a serial as bad as *Crossroads* are people who would not fight for a seat on the bus
  (Peter McKay, 6/8/80 Evening Standard*)*

The advantage of the addiction metaphor is that even if the reader is the viewer, because addiction is constructed as involuntary, the reader can concur with the condemnation of his or her habit. This model is used by both left and right, although the feminist presses would not express quite this contempt:

Perhaps its success is partly due to its timing – 4.30 being a particularly boring time for bored housewives who've got nothing to do but wait for their husbands to ring and tell them they'll be late at the office again!
  (Virginia Ironside, Daily Mail, *13/11/70)*

Soap opera is seen as the opium of the masses, particularly the female masses – soothing, deluding, product and producer of false consciousness. The other strategy – it's so bad it's good – could be called the kitsch strategy. The same features are commented on, but become cause for pleasure:

I am addicted to *Crossroads* (ATV) not for its virtues, which escape
me at the moment, but for its faults. I love it because of its warts, as it
were. An infatuation based on faults is difficult to cure...

(Nancy Banks-Smith, The Guardian, *8/8/72)*

Crucially, what both strategies do is avoid confronting the fact that
millions of people do enjoy, and take seriously, *Crossroads* and other
soap operas. It is unarguable that the production values of
Crossroads in particular are low. Hobson makes a clear argument
about why they are unlikely to improve. But to millions of fans
production values are clearly not the point – or at least not the main
point. I can spot shaky scenery, a muffed line, an odd shadow, as well
as the next fan. But what I watch for is different. It is partly a ritual
pleasure, which offers reassurance in its familiarity and regularity.
The credit sequence and theme tune are quite important here. Unlike
the 'hook' of the crime series – often up to three minutes of action before
the familiar break into the theme – the credits of *Brookside*,
Coronation Street and *Crossroads* all work primarily to establish a
sense of place. It is not character, in the sense of heroes and heroines,
or the promise of action, and enigmas resolved, that is central, but the
establishing of the 'where' – the place that we know, where life is
going on. And it is surely the predictable familiarity of the life
represented which pulls us in. Because all British soap operas have
some relation to realist conventions, the problems and worries of
characters are recognisable. We, too, live in the world of family
squabbles, demands for television licence fees and rising unemployment. It is not so much that 'life is like that' – it doesn't need
content analysis to establish that the more dramatic things happen
more often to more characters in soaps than 'in life' – but that the
generic lack of closure in combination with the realist premise, offers
a homology between soap-life and viewer life. Like us, soap opera
characters have to live with the consequences. It is usually only when
an actor or actress takes the option we haven't got and leaves the
programme, that there is any chance of a happy ending. Elsie may
have gone off to a golden sunset – but what comfort or hope is there
for Rita? Or Hilda? Or Mavis, Emily, Bet or Betty? And what has
Deidre settled for – the possibility that Ken will have an affair? Soap
opera characters are doomed to live out the truth of the old adage that
'No news is good news' – and no news is no soap.
    Of course this 'generic unhappiness' has its own counter-
balances. *Coronation Street* has increasingly dealt in comedy and
Crossroads has always had strong affiliations with the overdrive of
melodrama. *Brookside* relies mainly on the youth of many of its
characters, in combination with fairly regular celebrations and

location work. These emphases allow us to be entertained, to laugh and look, as well as think about life. I am not arguing that soap operas are tragic. Nor would I dispute that the way in which hope, happiness, a future, etc., are constructed within the programmes is very much within the ideological norms of Happiness = white middle-class heterosexual family unit (house owning). So, yes, sure, soaps must, at one level, work to reproduce the dominance of these norms – but this is only, in a way, to the extent that they provide a site for viewers to become involved in problems, issues and narratives that do touch on our own lives. You don't get involved with, or like, all of the characters – and quite often stories are not interesting or sympathetic. But that is part of the point.

© Charlotte Brunsdon
July 1984

Note

1.   Malcolm Hulke (1974) *Crossroads, a new beginning* (London), and other *Crossroads* novels. *Coronation Street* novels are by H. V. Kershaw, *The Crossroads Cookbook* by Hazel Adair and Peter Ling. London. 1977.
2.   *Ambridge: An English Village through the ages*, Jennifer Aldridge and John Tregorran. London. 1981.
3.   Rosalind Brunt discusses press coverage of soap opera very interestingly in 'Street Credibility' (*Marxism Today*, Dec. 1983)
4.   Dorothy Hobson (1982), *Crossroads, The Drama of a Soap Opera*. London.

Ian Connell

Fabulous Powers: Blaming the Media

There is now nothing remarkable, extraordinary, or arresting about the assertion that the media are biased and are to blame for the spread of this or that social problem by being carriers of all manner of distortion and misunderstanding. A view of the media along these lines is now commonplace.

It manages to remain so even although there have been several challenges to its adequacy as an explanation of how ideas, definitions, sentiments and the like circulate. These challenges refuse to accept that the media are as potent as is assumed in the claim that they are to blame. This claim rests on the assumption that the media can impose on *us*, or, win *our* acceptance of, not just particular ideas or emotions, but also entire ways of seeing and understanding quite outside of our everyday experience. We are, it seems, innocents unwittingly corrupted by our viewing and reading, and it is perhaps because of this ascription of innocence that such little headway has been made against these remarkably resilient, elegantly simple propositions. So robust are they that they now typically occur in speeches and critical essays as statements of fact, or as incontrovertible maxims in need of little, if any, proof, except perhaps, an illustration or two for those (few) who may yet be in some doubt.

If anything these views and assumptions will become even more difficult to dislodge as they become established principles of formal and informal education about the media. If the experience of our (twin) teenage sons is anything to go by, they would seem to be, at least as far as socialist education is concerned, principles to be learned early. Through their activities in youth CND they have come into contact with a variety of 'socialist' groups that hover on the edges of CND waiting to recruit new members. In the course of telling us about a recent 'educational' meeting run by one of the more 'revolutionary' of these groups, on the problems of developing socialism in Britain, the boys mentioned the media as one of the more pressing of these problems, because, owned as they are by capitalists, they must promote capitalist ideas. The reasoning was done for my benefit. I had interrupted their flow to ask why they thought the media constituted such a problem, but had I not, they sounded as if they would have continued without hesitation or pause. My interruption was initially received with a moment or two of stunned, perhaps incredulous, silence. They seemed unable to accept the possibility that I wasn't teasing them and that I might seriously not accept the status they had just conferred upon the media. Did they really have to explain such an elementary point? It seemed to them so evidently true that the media were biased and that this was a 'problem' that, having gathered their thoughts, they began their reply with 'Well, it's obvious...'

So, here they were, part of a new generation of socialists in the making, ready to endow the media with fabulous powers. So fabulous in fact, that some will now rank these media as one of and, sometimes, even as *the* mainstays of the present social fabric. This may seem a peculiarly left wing way of thinking about the media, but in fact it is not at all. It recognises no particular political affiliations. If the context is left wing, then it might be the *capitalist* media that are singled out, but those on the right (the Conservative party, say) and even those who would eschew any kind of overt political affiliations whatsoever (educationists worried about the effects of television on children, perhaps), are just as likely to do the same. The view that the media are biased and to blame for just about any troublesome state of affairs would seem to be a *popular* one. It has become, for many different kinds of groups, a nugget of wisdom, virtually impervious to criticism.

There is something markedly proverbial in the way in which this popular maxim is deployed, suggesting that when it occurs we are witnessing a myth at work. In his more general comments on the nature of mythology, Barthes suggested that myths are characterised by a number of properties. For example, they can abolish the complexity of human acts and can organise 'a world which is without contradictions because it is without depth, a world wide open and wallowing in the evident.' Furthermore, myths can displace the contingent, historical, fabricated quality of things social and, in so doing, can naturalise them. They can make social arrangements seem permanent, inescapably fixed, to be now, just as they have been always. While particular myths may accomplish more, in Barthes's view, all can do this much at least.

On the basis of Barthes's comments, a litmus test for whether something is a myth or not, would be whether it can perform that 'conjuring trick' which turns reality inside-out, which empties it of history and fills it with nature instead. In other words, to draw a veil over the fact that our relations with one another are our products, just as much as our commodities. If the view we have been discussing really is to be classed as a myth, then it, too, must be capable of this cultural alchemy.

During the course of the miners' strike such accusations were frequently directed at the media, and at journalism in particular. They differed from those made in other situations in very few respects, though perhaps feelings about the media during this exceptionally long, bitter and, at times, brutal dispute were somewhat stronger than usual. Those on strike and involved in picketing felt so strongly that the media were double-dealing that direct action was taken against a number of TV crews as they attempted to record, for example, mounted police charging picket lines. Very quickly newsrooms made a point of including their personnel on the injured lists. Inevitably, reference to the media was a regular feature of the speeches made by the leadership of the NUM and the NCB. While Mr. Scargill began for a time to refer to journalists as vermin, Mr. McGregor could only just manage to remain courteous about the intervention of press proprietor Robert Maxwell.

On each side of the dispute the media were assumed to be a dangerously potent force whose effectivity was unquestioned. Without any shadow of doubt, and without any evidence beyond fragments of remembered words and images, those charging the media with bias did so because they felt they really were influential, and really did shape people's view of the dispute. As in other instances, no evidence was actually required. Those involved took as a statement of fact the assertion that they were up against a potent propaganda machine.

This assumes quite a bit about the reception of stories by those not directly involved. The media *may* indeed have played some part in shaping people's views of the dispute but, whether they did or not will depend upon just how the relevant programmes were watched and/or read. Did people give their undivided attention to viewing or listening to news bulletins, for instance? Despite widespread notions that people are 'glued to the box', watching TV is *normally* done in conjunction with at least one other activity and people do not *normally* watch every moment of programmes. When attention was given, did people find what they saw, heard, or read, comprehensible? If they found it so, did they also find it agreeable, or did they suspect it to be, in one way or another, partial, or to confirm their 'worst fears'? These are only some of the questions to which answers would have to be found before we could say the media had played a part in ... and what that part was. This *cannot* be decided on the basis of the *combatants'* viewing alone.

Another problem with the view that the media are to blame is that it makes it easy to think that the media present meanings already produced, packaged and ready for immediate consumption. It obscures the fact that when we actually watch the news, or bits of it, we *too* are involved in making meanings, with resources drawn from previous encounters with the media, certainly, but also from all the other aspects of our lives. The very existence of *definite* views about this or that situation depends not just on the media's contributions, but also upon our *active* involvement. We, as viewers, are not at all the passive bystanders, innocent or otherwise, that the myth makes us out to be.

The assertion followed much the same sort of pattern during the miners' strike as it does on other occasions. It would usually occur at that moment when the developing situation presented unforeseen difficulties and problems, or when events took what seemed to the protagonists to be unexpected and perplexing turns. In the course of this dispute there were a number of developments that had hitherto been considered unthinkable, impossible even. There were contingencies like the lack of success in the use of the 'flying' and 'mass' picket and the quite astounding determination and resolve of those on strike, which seemed to strengthen with each attempt by either Government, police or NCB to undermine them. But perhaps the most telling was the failure to obtain decisive action in support of the NUM's case. 'Calls' for such action went unheeded. Not only was the support for the strike among miners less than unanimous, there was also little wholehearted secondary support, little solidarity to be summoned up just when it was deemed necessary.

These contingencies were threatening. The actions of workers in other areas signified that, in a sense, the 'labour movement' was out of control and that the leadership was left with only formal authority and an empty rhetoric as 'their men' failed to do as they were told. The invocation of the media as to blame, as the malevolent manipulator of moderate minds, merely served to obscure, none too well, just how these strained relations between leaders and the (reluctantly) led had developed. It was quite evident that the media did not operate merely to put the miners' case. (They themselves were not above employing a myth or two in their accounts of the strike.) Since they were not explicitly *for* the miners, nor any other group of workers when in dispute, they could be made to seem explicitly *against* them.

Blaming the media may have deflected criticism directed at the leadership of the NUM and of the TUC, and may have made it easier to live with uncomfortable facts. As in other situations, it certainly helped to melt away some of the complexities which developing situations present, and to absolve those upon whom blame might, readily and rightly, have been placed. What chance was there of success against so powerful a force as the media, a force which can so easily seem a law unto itself, accountable to no-one except, perhaps, its political masters? When such might as they possess is directed against the labour movement and its leaders, is it really any wonder that solidarity crumbles? This fundamental principle – solidarity – can, it seems, resist many things. It can, apparently, even emerge unscathed from the attempts by unions to encourage open competition between workers over the price at which they are prepared to sell their skills. What it cannot withstand, however, is 'unfair interference' from outside. Media interference, it seems, has the power to mute calls in the name of solidarity and brotherhood, to muddle the membership and to set 'brother' against 'brother'. Everything is, then, made to hinge on control of this source of interference; hence, Arthur Scargill's suggestion that there should be fifteen minutes per week turned over on TV to presenting the miners' case.

Control of the media is an important matter, but its pursuit can deflect attention from 'internal' relations and the actions in the course of which they arise and develop. Genuine solidarity requires something more than ritual incantation in stirring speeches at moments of crisis, to a chorus of 'Arthur Scargill . . . we'll support you evermore.' If, in the course of this dispute, the media's stories really did undermine solidarity, then we can only conclude that the foundations of this solidarity were already shaky, thanks to such activities as inter-union rivalry and wage competition and, moreover, to the remoteness and lack of accountability of union leaders who have increasingly seemed to members not to represent their views. In short, if the stories did something of the sort, it was because they touched already tender nerves. To blame the media again might be tempting, but it would be to refuse to acknowledge *what else* inhibits the development of solidarity. Furthermore, it would again leave open a space for others, the present Government among them, to step in and further develop the sense of alienation from the 'labour movement' which many now experience.

As with any other myth that we do not feel or live, it can be easy to be critical. It is worth reminding ourselves, therefore, that while we may not be held by a particular myth or myths, some myths certainly do touch all our lives. Clearly, living is easier and more straight-forward if we can abolish uncomfortable facts by, as it were, sweeping them under the carpet or by blaming them on somebody else. We may even be aware, in doing something of the sort, that it is not really an adequate solution, just the best possible that we can come up with in the circumstances. Myths (the one I have been discussing as much as any other) enable us to avoid coming to terms with our own part, our own involvement, in making things as they are. In the end, myths can make it seem that we have nothing to do with the course of anything so grand as history; it just happens, or is made by others while we enjoy, suffer, or make the best of, the results. It is not too difficult to think of times when the media have made us angry or have made us consider their influence on others. That said, however, we shall need to be careful about 'blaming' the media. While it may be comforting to do so, it explains too little and obscures too much. The trouble with blaming the media is that it pulls them out of context, sometimes minimising their influence and, at other times, inflating it out of all proportion. We should not ignore the media and we should certainly not see them as blameless. The stories they put about can be all the things they are normally accused of – trivial, biased, personalised, sensational, sexist and boringly incomprehensible. It has to be said, however, that they can also be usefully informative and enlightening, though this is rarely emphasised in critical work. But, just what their role is in a given situation depends, to an extent considerably greater than has till now been allowed, on what viewers and readers bring to, and make of, these stories. *If* stories have been influential or persuasive, *if* they have consolidated particular interpretations, then it can only be because they have connected with feelings and thoughts that are already in place. The suggestion that these feelings and thoughts have simply been imposed on the audience by biased media is, really, little more than a convenient fiction that allows us to avoid confronting the difficulties that arise once we acknowledge our involvement.

The 'A' Team: Paradigms of Masculinity

Finally the crisis of representation ends. At the *'A' Team*. Its apparent meaning as an inferior, off-the-shelf Hollywood authoritarian-as-outlaw pastiche is undercut, to the point of self-laceration, by a deeply subversive interior eschatology. At the head of this 'unholy' Trinity is the ominous *pater familias* Hannibal Smith (acted by the grizzled George Peppard whom we half-remember as the original Luftwaffe's *Blue Max*). He is held in a permanently renegotiated bargain of duplicity with his 'team' (Foucaultians will not miss the homophilic overtones) of B.A., a molten mass of black insubordination held in a masochistic self-discipline as demanding as Réage's 'O' (to which he obliquely refers in the trope 'No pain, no gain') and the deluded lovers, Face and Murdock. But this uneasy triptych of sexual power, each atomised constituent of which continually edges towards insubordination, escape or simple suicide, transmogrifies, on threat, into a force as highly-strung as an isosceles triangle. And in the process taughtens its spiral of sexual nuance near to vertigo.

Everything is stated before the game begins. The clowns of sub-Trotskyist 'aesthetics' miss all this with their unbearably trite 'turn that rubbish off and I'll read you some *Swallows and Amazons* mentality. For here, A-Teamed, is the very iconography of subordination: Murdock with, as it were, his very super-ego miniaturised in the Imryesque modules of post-plastic he carries round his belt; BA, the best car wax advertiser since *The Buddha*, an infinite condensation of that hypnotised will which haunts the B-sides of so much of the rap-scratch-Malcolm stuff; and that conceptual full-stop, the classic 'Hugh Hefner-type', Face.

To try and clear the conceptual air, I felt impelled to open a new space in this dense discussion with Jesse Ash, Reader in Comparative Television with a particular interest in Image/Text problems and Tom Ryan of Cardiff, whose pioneering work on Latent Homosexuality in *Starsky and Hutch* anticipated later feminist work on *Cagney and Lacey*. William Atkinson has contributed a footnote on some of the neo-psychiatric and international issues raised in our conversation. The discussion commences with a bald and hopefully 'enabling' formulation :

DW: Why do you like the *'A' Team*?

TR: Because they are good trickers. Like they make good set-ups. They make plans so that the baddies who are after the *'A'-Team* get caught in a net and things like that.

DW: I am continually struck by the team's almost voluptuous sense of decorum.

JA: Well, they were in the military army and they escaped. That's why everyone is after them, you see. Because they were the best people in the war. They are outlaws, so they hide most of the time. They were on an aeroplane but they pretended to have crashed. And they made their car blow up.

DW: So in a Frankfurtian sense they rebel against repressive tolerance.

TR: The *'A' Team* live together between episodes. I don't think they have a house. They sleep in bushes and stuff. Hannibal likes fishing. That's how they start adventures. They're in a pub, say, and the baddies come along and karate all the people that are in. And the *'A' Team* come and see the whole place. Then they have a drink. Then the baddies come in. That's how they start the fight.

DW: Perhaps you would like to comment at this early stage on the notion, put most starkly by Dee Dee Glass, of the inevitability of a separatisation and thus fetishisation of women's culture . . . given the *'A' Team*'s sense of its own audience.

JA: Amy is quite nice. She's the girl in the *'A' Team*. Of course, there has to be a girl in the *'A' Team*. She wasn't in the war, though. They met when she went shopping or something. No, when they went swimming. And they came out, oh yeah, and they met her on a boat. They *met*.

DW: Obviously my own work on sexual dissonance and male masochism would want to stress the erotic dynamics of the *'A' Team*. Where would you locate these?

TR: Murdock is really crazy. Most of the time he's in the back of the van. He keeps saying, 'Oh, my God, please help me, now I must be in big trouble, I need some X-ray eyes.' He's a brilliant fighter. Once there was a karate one. He went pee, pwish and whoosh in the karate's eyes. Crump, ugh.

JA: I like BA the best. In the film he's called two names. He's called BA in the film but his real name is Mr. T. He's fantastically strong and he doesn't say very much. He mostly says 'Move it, sucker,' to

Murdock for being stupid. Then Murdock says to BA, 'You better not do that, sucker,' back. He just copies B.A., see B.A. respects Hannibal, see. Sometimes he just does what he wants to, sometimes he says to Hannibal, 'I'll do whatever you say.' Face is always in his little car, a white car with red lines. Face's relationship with B.A. is quite a problem. He really can't get on.

DW: One senses powerfully, doesn't one, the hubris which lies within the jouissance. Is that tension heightened by the Team's deliberate inaccessibility, do you think?

TR: You have to *know* the *'A' Team* to get them to help you. They don't have a phone number. At the very first that's what it says. 'If you can find them, get the *'A' Team'*. You *can* write a letter. But never ask the police. The police would be furious if you asked them because they want to get the money for the *'A' Team* which is about 40 billion pounds. It's better when the *'A' Team* arrest you! The *'A' Team* are better than Superman because they are a *team.*

DW: I recently heard one of our ouvrierist comrades attempting to legitimise watching the *'A' Team* by some convoluted parallel to a group of striking miners in Mardy who had adopted the name 'The A Team'. How does that sort of syndicalist syllogism strike you? Dr. Ryan, you have a special knowledge of the Welsh conceptual experience.

TR: Well, they would have to have big blokes who are really smart and all that. About twenty. They'd have to make *'A' Team* set-ups. Say there's a rope here and the police are walking down and plisht, they are tucked up by the string like that and then they'd make all the nets fall down on the scabs. And they'd have to copy from the *'A' Team* on television to make plans like the *'A' Team* set-ups. They'd have to have ropes and special equipment in the van. They would have to have someone like Face, who usually gets the engines they need for a particular job.

JA: I hope the miners win and mash up Mrs. Thatcher. If I met them I would get their autographs. I'd like to be in the *'A' Team* too, but if I was in it, it would be the 'B' Team or the 'C' Team.

DW: Jameson says of Barthes, 'He taught us to read with our bodies – and often write with them as well.' How do you connect that remarkable insight with the *'A' Team* as a *visual* text?

JA: I liked the bit, it was the last one of the old series. Well, what it was was that there were these Chinese fighters who were really mad and doing all this karate stuff and, of course, the *'A' Team* did it too. They were getting this Chinese restaurant into a bad place. They were mashing it up. They wanted all the money that it had, it was quite a rich restaurant. There was an old man and they shot the old man.

TR: Amy's friend got them help!

JA: Then there was one where Murdock and Face had to take a door off and they made a gun with one of them holders and the baddies came chasing along with their guns and the *'A' Team* were in the helicopter. Hannibal had the gun and he was firing through the door into the beach and when they went on there was a mountain. And Murdock and Hannibal went up the side of the mountain. Just missed it, like that. And the guns went crick, clack. But the enemy was going round the rock, but he went too near it and it beat up. Good one, that.

DW: Doesn't one have to accept, to embrace even, the role of pistol-penis in the *'A' Team* sensorium?

TR: The *'A' Team* is spot on. In *T. J. Hooker* there's always violence and too many guns, but the *'A' Team* only use guns when they are definitely in trouble. *T. J. Hooker* uses guns all the time. Whatever he does, he's holding it in his hand. Even if there is no one answering the gun, he still holds it in his hand.

JA: Remember that film where he shot the person just to kill it and he says to Romano, 'Well, that just goes to show.'

JR: The army has guns, too, but there are not many army films except at Christmas and holidays. There's lots of guns on holidays. *Chips* has thousands of guns.

JA: What's the name again, with the girl with tight trousers, *Dukes of Hazard*, they haven't got guns but they fight all the time and crash the cars up.

DW: Without getting bogged down in issues of intertextuality, what is, for you, the key to the *'A' Team*'s self-referential structure?

TR: They make quite excellent plans and that's how they explain it out and they stand to get how you feel and you know.

JA: I'd say that question's easy. You've read a lot about the *'A' Team* but all you need to say is that it's better than all the other programmes because it's got more silliness in it. Face is quite happy and always falling in swimming pools and jumping off drawbridges and doing all those stupid things and B.A.'s always being tough and Murdock's always copying him and Hannibal keeps on saying, 'Stop it,' and they're not stopping it.

William Atkinson was not able to participate in the discussion since he was doing *'A' Team* source work in Los Angeles at the time of our meeting. He, however, adds, 'I like it because they've got good tricks and they are good fighters and you only have to phone them up. They help people who need help. I like B.A. because he's black and not many fighters on TV are. He gets cross, in his mind, and then he wants his tummy to go ugh, ugh. But he can't do it with his brain. That's what happens to me sometimes when I'm at school and I don't want to do this piece of work but Miss says I have to. B.A. understands how to concentrate your brain.'

Len Masterman

The Battle of Orgreave

'What is noted,' Barthes observed, 'is by definition notable.' The most notable features of the current miners' dispute, television implicitly assures us, are picket violence (indisputably there, night after night, on our screens) and the problems facing the police in trying to keep order in difficult and often impossible situations. The angle from which events are seen sharpens our apparently 'natural' sympathy for working miners, who are intimidated as they go to the pit, and for a police force trying to keep the peace in a dispute in which they themselves have no direct interest. Television positions us, familiarly, behind police lines. The stones and bricks hurled at the police are also aimed at us. *We* are on the receiving end of the angry cries of 'scabs' and 'bastards' as we accompany working miners through the police cordon. In these circumstances it is scarcely surprising that even the leader of the Labour Party should be willing to accept the agenda set by television and condemn 'picket line violence' (the current euphemism for 'picket violence').

A de-mythologising television criticism, however, can never be content to analyse only what is on the screen. It must necessarily dwell upon what has been excluded as inappropriate. It must concern itself, that is, with television's structured absences: the images which lie on the cutting room floor, the events which are disregarded, and the perspectives which are never considered. One does not have to enquire very deeply into the miners' dispute to discover that police violence and intimidation are very much live issues and are, indeed, topics of major concern in many mining communities. And one does not have to be inordinately suspicious to suggest that the persistent absence from media accounts of *this* aspect of the strike may constitute a sanitising operation of considerable proportions.

By its very nature, evidence of television's absences is difficult for viewers to establish. But ITN's coverage of events at the Orgreave coking plant in South Yorkshire in June 1984, a rare example of the reporting of police violence by television, succeeded in throwing into sharp relief strategic omissions from the BBC's account of the same events.

BBC 1's early evening news on June 18th opened with the Orgreave story. Behind the newsreader, Moira Stewart, was projected a blow-up of a single violent image: a man, presumably a miner, taking a running kick at a policeman (see p. 101). The image functioned emblematically. Chosen from all the footage available as *the* symbol of what Orgreave signified, the film extract of miners attacking the police from which this image was taken was to be shown again and again on BBC programmes over the next week. It is a sequence which will, no doubt, continue to be circulated by the BBC whenever the events at Orgreave are represented for future generations.

Moira Stewart's scene-setting introduction and John Thorne's on-the-spot report develop three strong themes: the military-style planning of the operation by Arthur Scargill, the miners' leader, (illustrated with a somewhat sinister black-and-white photograph of him 'directing operations' by two-way radio); doubt over whether head injuries sustained by Scargill were actually inflicted by the police (it is even implied that he may have been hit over the head by one of his own stone-throwing pickets); and the essentially defensive and reactive nature of the police's role in the conflict. Moira Stewart:

'Over 5,000 pickets at Orgreave fought a pitched battle with over two thousand police and the latest tally was 93 arrests, 28 policemen and at least 51 pickets injured. Mr. Scargill, who had been directing operations on a two-way radio, was later found sitting on a kerb looking stunned after policemen with riot shields had run by under a hail of stones. Ambulancemen treated his head injury and then helped him to an ambulance which took him to hospital where he is being kept overnight. He believes (original emphasis) he was hit by a riot shield. A senior police officer says (my emphasis) he saw him slip off a bank and hit his head on a sleeper but doesn't know whether he'd already been injured.'

John Thorne's eye witness report is reproduced on p. 107 (column one). It was accompanied by film in which it was clear that, whatever the pickets' planning, the police operations were organised with some precision to develop through specific phases (massed ranks to prevent pickets pushing forward; cavalry charges for dispersal; riot police for quick arrests). Thorne's words, 'The attacks on individual policemen were horrific. The police commanders said it was a marvel that no one was killed,' were exemplified by disturbing footage (from which the opening still image was taken) of policemen being kicked. The violence at Orgreave was presented unequivocally as picket violence ('It appeared to be a conscious decision to use any method to stop the coke lorries') with picketing turning to rioting and destruction, and the police compelled to act defensively to retain

Establishing the meaning of Orgreave: BBC early evening news, 18/6/1984.

control under 'tremendous pressure'.

And there the matter might have remained, as it does on most other evenings, neatly packaged and disposed of by broadcasters who have few inhibitions about telling their audiences what to think and make little attempt to provide viewers with a range of evidence from which they might draw their own conclusions. The report fitted into the predictable pattern adopted by the BBC in its routine coverage of the dispute.*

This evening, however, was to be different. For ITN's coverage of Orgreave showed images of a very different complexion. Phil Roman's report and the images accompanying it make clear that some of the worst violence, an escalation from the pushing and stone-throwing, was administered by heavily-armed riot police upon anyone whom they could catch. Morevoer, this was not done in the heat of the moment but as part of a planned operation. The decision to 'turn nasty' was one deliberately made by the police. The film showed the police lines opening up, the horses galloping into a group of pickets, who were simply standing around, and the riot police following up wielding their truncheons. The police were '*taking advantage* (my emphasis) of the confusion caused by the horses... The pickets knew what to expect. They had been warned that it could turn nasty, and it did.'

The images which followed turned Orgreave into one of the biggest media stories of the entire strike. One of them showed a policeman repeatedly clubbing a fallen man to the head in a manner familiar within the context of Chile or South Africa but never before seen on television being administered by British policemen upon British workers. Nor is it clear that this was an isolated incident. An arrested miner being frog-marched behind police lines yells to the camera-crew, 'You want to get in there and see what they're doing.' During the worst of the beatings most of the pickets ran away, but some ran across to help colleagues who were being truncheoned. The *direction* in which they were running, the same as that of the 'violent' miners in the BBC film, suggests that the 'horrific' violence attributed to the miners by the BBC was carried out in defence of beleaguered colleagues.

---

*It is interesting to note that, in this respect, though presumably reported independently of one another, the Orgreave stories run by BBC radio's *The World At One*, and *BBC Television News* have far more in common with one another than they have with what soon came to be seen as the most significant events at Orgreave. Were BBC radio and television reporters receiving common guidance from above in their coverage of the strike? If so, it is, again, the study of significant textual absences which is likely to give the clearest indication of the nature of that guidance.

The ITN footage raises serious questions about the BBC's coverage of Orgreave. Many commentators over the next few days were to remark upon the disturbing images of police violence 'which we all saw on TV'. None made the point that no such images were transmitted on BBC television. Did the BBC crew simply fail to shoot any images of police violence? Examination of the BBC film reveals that the camera *was covering* the key sequence of events when the riot police moved in. Close comparison of BBC and ITN footage shows that the BBC film has in shot the man who was most severely beaten by the police, but that *the film has been cut at precisely the point when the policeman begins to set about him with his truncheon.* What we cut away to are miners' retaliatory attempts to help their colleagues. But because the BBC film has not shown any examples of police violence, these de-contextualised images can only signify *unprovoked* violence by pickets.

The charge against BBC Television News of suppressing references to police violence at Orgreave is a serious one. It is not the case that events at Orgreave caught the BBC camera crew by surprise. They must have been fully alerted to the stepping up of preparations behind police lines (the mustering of the horses and the riot police), and, indeed, as we have seen, they were shooting during the key sequence of events. But even if no images of the riot police in action had been captured, what possible reason could there be for omitting any reference to the extraordinary scenes of police violence from the commentary? During the key 'riot police' sequence, the BBC commentary speaks, simply, of 'hand-to-hand' fighting and of 'horrific' attacks upon policemen only. That this account misleadingly distorted the events which actually took place was to be implicitly acknowledged, as we shall see, by changes made to this commentary by the main *BBC Nine O'clock News* later the same evening.

For all watchers of the BBC's way with industrial disputes, the discussion on Orgreave in *Sixty Minutes*, following the early evening news is, in the light of the ITN footage, a collector's piece. The discussants were presenter Nick Ross, Jack Taylor, leader of the South Yorkshire miners and Eldon Griffiths, Parliamentary Spokesperson for the Police Federation.

Nick Ross: Mr. Taylor, how on earth do you explain what happened at Orgreave today?

Jack Taylor: Well, I think you should be asking that question to police, not just asking it to me. They were in a position today where we saw scenes that we... well, I thought we'd never see them in Britain. We had people on horses, policemen, riding into crowds of miners with batons swinging. We had policemen with dogs, we had policemen by the thousand there. It's O.K. you saying to me how can I explain it. I'll tell you what, everyone seems to assume that it was equal. What we had was miners in tee-shirts and jeans and running pumps. And we had police in shin-guards with riot shields, with long staves, attacking working people.

Nick Ross: Mr. Taylor, can I just get this right for people who saw the news footage earlier? Your interpretation of what happened is that 5,000 miners, striking miners, were peacefully picketing. The police then stormed the picketing miners.

Jack Taylor: Today there we had a situation where policemen were really *beating* (original emphasis) miners. Now if they believe they can beat us into submission as well as starve us into submission, they don't understand us.

Nick Ross: Well, some people, Mr. Taylor, will certainly agree with what you say. I suspect that the vast majority will be *astonished* (original emphasis) at hearing your account, particularly since there are so many reports from independent witnesses. I've got one here, for example, from a garage owner nearby who says that the pickets smashed his doors, took three of his cars and set them alight – so many independent people are saying that it was pickets who were running amok, not the police.

Jack Taylor: I'll tell you what, I was there. I was there, and I can tell you what I saw. I saw policemen . . . in fact I was chased along a road 300 yards myself and the problem is if you were the back one you got a beating. I were pulled by the hair to the ground, and if you want witnesses I can bring you witnesses to say that was right. Now if you are telling me that is the sort of country that you and me are looking forward to for the rest of our lives, I'll tell you what we want to have a re-look.

Nick Ross: . . . In our Westminster studio is Eldon Griffiths, Tory M.P., who is Parliamentary Spokesman for the Police Federation. You heard that Mr. Griffiths – what is your assessment of what happened today?

Eldon Griffiths: I think you used the right word and you said it was astonishing that Mr. Taylor should paint a picture of the police attacking the pickets . . .

Poor Nick Ross. With only the inadequate BBC coverage to rely on for guidance he fails to see the real story of Orgreave, even though

Taylor places it in his lap. Taylor's account, vivid though it is, is given little credence by Ross. Indeed, in telling his story at all, Taylor has to break with the pre-formulated framework placed upon the discussion by Ross. For Taylor has been invited to the studio to be called to account, to justify to the nation the inexplicable: 'How on earth do you explain what happened at Orgreave today?' Interestingly, Taylor doesn't simply break with Ross's framework, he suggests how Ross might more profitably conduct the discussion – by addressing his question to the police. This advice, of course, is ignored by Ross when Griffiths is eventually brought into the discussion. Indeed, the invitation to Griffiths to give 'your assessment of what happened today' is notably open and generous in contrast with the treatment accorded to Taylor.

Throughout the Orgreave coverage the differential credibility accorded to police representatives and miners as sources is revealing. The miner's *eye-witness* story is dismissed as astonishing, whilst the police spokesperson is asked in all seriousness for his assessment of a situation at which he was not present. Similarly, the police statement that Scargill 'slipped' in injuring his head, far from being challenged by reporters, is privileged against Scargill's mere 'claims' that he was struck by a riot shield.

Jack Taylor's account, which is dismissed out of hand by Ross is, in fact, corroborated by the ITN images shown earlier (and one can reasonably surmise that those images themselves may have been merely the tip of a very unsavoury iceberg). Jack Taylor's account also homed-in on what were soon to be acknowledged, even by the police, as the central issues of Orgreave, and generally came considerably closer to conveying the most important story from the picket line than did the BBC's own reports. A fundamental criticism of BBC coverage of Orgreave, then, is a journalistic one: that in their eagerness to select and shape events to fit a preformulated interpretation, they missed by a mile what was to become the main story of Orgreave. Finally, that a BBC interviewer and a spokesperson for the Police Federation should put an *identical* interpretation upon events at which they were not present, and that they should do so in the face of evidence from an eye-witness who was himself a victim of police harassment is, to put it charitably, striking.

The version of Orgreave constructed by the early BBC news and *Sixty Minutes* soon lay in tatters. By the time of transmission of BBC's *Nine o'clock News* it had become clear that more powerful alternative images of Orgreave were in circulation. Peter Sissons on *Channel Four News* at seven o'clock had confronted the Chief Constable of South Yorkshire directly: 'We've seen pictures of policemen clearly losing their tempers and using their truncheons. Do policemen truncheoning miners to the ground risk disciplinary proceedings?' The story was developing by the hour, and pointing up embarrassing lacunae in the BBC's account.

In order to cope with what was fast becoming a crisis of credibility, the *Nine O'Clock News* made a number of significant changes to its commentary (see opposite page) to give greater emphasis to police violence. New additions to the commentary described the police as handing out 'as much physical punishment as they received,' whilst 'the riot squads gave no quarter,' and, in a deathless phrase, used 'their batons liberally.' For the first time, too, there was a suggestion that the police were responsible for escalating the violence, the sending in of riot squad reinforcements being described as

'the trigger for some of the worst violence to this lengthy dispute.'

The notion that the strikers' blockade was planned like a 'military' operation, a key theme of the early coverage, is dropped. And consider the following: in the early news,

'The attacks on individual policemen were horrific. The police commanders said it was a marvel that no-one was killed'

has become, by nine o'clock:

'The attacks on policemen were horrific but the riot squads gave no quarter, using their batons liberally. "It was a miracle no-one was killed," said one police commander.'

The meaning of the police statement has been completely changed, so that now it is the riot squads and not the pickets who are said to be (inadvertently?) endangering lives. Finally, the emblematic still image at the beginning of the early news, *the* dominant symbol of Orgreave at six o'clock has, by nine, been for the time being discreetly dropped.

The changes reveal the extent to which news presentation is an ideological construction, rather than a matter of unproblematic reporting. For the changes in the meaning of Orgreave over a relatively short period of time were provoked not by events on the picket line, but by pressures from elsewhere. It is noteworthy, however, that these changes occurred largely at the level of the story's surface meanings. Its deeper structures remained largely intact. Though additional references to aggressive police tactics had been woven into the text, there was no explicit condemnation (or even mild disapproval) of police action, and no acknowledgement that unnecessary police violence was the central issue at stake. But that

BBC TELEVISION NEWS COMMENTARIES
FROM ORGREAVE, MONDAY, JUNE 18th, 1984,
by John Thorne
(Major differences are indicated in bold type)

5.40 NEWS

The strikers' blockade was planned like a **military** operation with miners arriving from all over the country. But the police responded with speed matching the 5,000 pickets with thousands of their own forces.

At first police horses tried to shepherd the miners out of the convoy road. The violence reached a new peak as miners surged forward against the riot shields. Police **fought** with truncheons* under a barrage of stones and missiles. By mid-morning the picketing had turned to rioting.

The police hadn't lost ground, but more riot squads were needed as **reinforcements** in the front line **as the pressure increased**. Eventually senior officers ordered in the mounted police **to disperse the miners**. A gap opened and the horses galloped in.

Police horses are the most feared weapon in the present armoury.

But it's the riot squads that follow up to make the arrests and today on the fields around Orgreave the police became involved in some of the most vicious hand-to-hand fighting of the entire miners' dispute. The attacks on individual policemen were horrific. The police commanders said it was a marvel that no-one was killed. The battle lasted throughout the morning, and in all police made over 100 arrests as the **scuffles** ebbed and flowed...

At all times the police were in control but under tremendous pressure. There was never anything peaceful about the front line confrontation.

It appeared to be a conscious decision to use any method to stop the coke lorries.

NINE O'CLOCK NEWS

The strikers' blockade of Orgreave was a precisely planned operation but the police responded, **sending in riot squad reinforcements** to match the 5,000 or more pickets.

And that was **the trigger for some of the worst violence of this lengthy dispute**. It reached a peak as miners surged forward against the riot shields. Policemen **hit out** with truncheons* under a barrage of stones and missiles. Mass picketing had turned to rioting.

The police didn't give any ground and **on the front line they handed out as much physical punishment as they received**. Eventually the senior officer ordered in the mounted police. A gap opened in the ranks and the horses galloped in. The horses are the most feared weapon in the police armoury on the picket line and they are very effective. But it's the riot squads that follow-up to make the arrests, and today on the fields **of battle** around Orgreave the police were involved in some of the most vicious hand-to-hand fighting of the entire miners' dispute. The attacks on policemen were horrific **but the riot squads gave no quarter using their batons liberally**. 'It was a miracle no-one was killed,' said one police commander.

At all times the police were in control. There were over 100 arrests as the **fighting** ebbed and flowed...

---

* References to a relatively innocuous incident in the film in which a policeman on the front line uses a trunchon as the pickets press forward.

was the big story of Orgreave and it was to force itself irresistibly to the centre of the stage over the next few days.*

What is the significance of the sorry catalogue of suppression, timorousness and misreporting which characterised the BBC's early coverage of Orgreave? It is a reminder that what is omitted from television's agenda cannot easily enter the *general* consciousness and that the control of information, whether it takes a brutal or sophisticated form, is the very cornerstone of political power. In an obvious way, television's version of Orgreave is yet another addition to the plump dossier of documented cases of the BBC's hostility to industrial action by trade unionists. It is another example of the corporation's persistent Reithean awareness, in times of social and political crisis, of its broader social 'responsibilities'. Orgreave, too, demonstrates Dallas Smythe's thesis that television's prime economic and ideological function is to produce not programmes but *audiences*, large numbers of people who will, it is hoped, buy a particular product or support particular social or political policies. As we have seen, public figures can now make unproblematic short-hand reference to picket violence, and be easily and widely understood because a large audience familiar with that view *has already been summoned into existence* by the media.

But perhaps the most significant consequence of the kind of reporting exemplified by the BBC at Orgreave lies in its implications for future communications policy in Britain. Whilst it will become increasingly important to argue over the next decade against the growing privatisation of information, and the increasing colonisation of broadcasting by commercial interests, the case for public service broadcasting is immeasurably weakened by an existing model which predominantly serves established interests. The gap which has opened up between the reality of paternalistic 'public service' broadcasting and the possibility of a broadcasting service which would be genuinely in the public interest is a debilitating one for those

---

*For example, on June 19th, the day after Orgreave, all of the main BBC radio news programmes, as well as both BBC and ITN early evening television news, considered the implications of what Sir Robin Day described as 'some particularly disturbing shots which *seemed* to show one policeman striking a picket several times across the head with a truncheon' (original emphasis). Only *Sixty Minutes* again evaded the issue by amplifying a story picked up from some of the morning papers on the alleged concern of the Queen at picket line violence. This item took the form of an interview with Norman St. John Stevas, who blew the gaff by confessing that this 'story' did not originate from a reliable source, and did not amount to 'very much more than gossip'. In view of the programme's stance the previous evening, it was perhaps too much to expect it to confront directly the issue of police violence. But to miss the mark so widely on successive evenings is a sad commentary on the quality of the programme's coverage of the event.

attempting to develop a unified strategy against the monopoly of broadcasting by market forces. Given the record of the BBC, few people involved in or sympathetic towards the labour movement can be expected to leap to its defence. Indeed, the movement was much better served at Orgreave by a commercial news organisation which at least has to take some account of the interests of its customers, than it was by an avowedly public service organisation. Orgreave is a salutary reminder, then, that arguing for public service broadcasting involves not simply defending the BBC, but changing it. And if that proves impossible, it will mean looking to entirely new models to serve the public interest. The immediate victims of the BBC's coverage of Orgreave were the striking miners. But the most significant long-term casualty of television coverage of the miners' dispute may well turn out to be the BBC itself.

Kevin Robins & Frank Webster

Today's Television and Tomorrow's World

The detection of food contamination; *in vitro* fertilisation; a safety
device for climbing pylons; alternatives to coal and oil; unblocking
irrigation pipes; the functions of vitamin E; the secret of Japanese
technological and industrial success; motorway surveillance; the
detection of contraband fruit in California (the 'smuggled banana');
voice synthesis; ink jet printing; 'flu vaccine; computer music. Just
some of the varied issues covered by *Tomorrow's World* in May, 1984.
Fragments of 'reality' randomly collated into a mosaic image of our
scientific and technological future. A farrago of the serious, the trivial
and the eccentric – all presented as being equally worthy of our
attention.

To bring us tidings of our impending future no effort is spared.
The *Tomorrow's World* team scans and patrols the world to bring us
reports from the cutting edge of 'progress' (along with the actuality
footage that will confirm and authenticate them). No effort is spared
to produce dramatic effects and increase viewer involvement. The
team is ready to fly and fall and climb and dive on our behalf like
peak-time *Blue Peter* presenters. Back in the studio, the team weave
an agile path through a landscape of complex diagrams and imposing
models (chips, ovaries, brains and molecules). And all the while they
keep up an authoritative, fluent and friendly patter.

And what is the end result? Firstly, there is a distinct *trivialisation*
of many of the topics covered, as entertainment comes to prevail over
information. The viewer, it is assumed, is not too bright, perhaps
tired after a day's work, and probably unconcerned about science and
technology anyway. Maybe he or she is only waiting for *Top of the
Pops*. So the issues must be put across in an attractive and
entertaining way. They must be little pellets of information in quick
succession, easy and enjoyable to consume. There must be no talking
heads, as much location shooting as the budget allows, and plenty of
audio-visual illustrations. The programme becomes a show, a
performance, and science and technology are turned into a spectacle
– visual, humorous and enjoyable. So Peter Macann dangles from the
top of a pylon and Judith Hann is electronically transposed into a
prehistoric landscape, complete with model dinosaurs. Exploring the

world of science and technology can be great fun. And isn't it a funny world we live in, anyway? Truth can be stranger than fiction. Who would have thought of linking a firefly's glowing tail with the detection of contamination in food? And fancy coconuts being used in the extraction of gold! A kangaroo-proof fence in the Australian outback! Waterproof paper?! Just amazing!

Tomorrow's World sets out to fascinate, to surprise, to astonish and amaze. It is a shop window regaled with sleek new inventions and technological toys. But the consequence of this gee-whizz enthusiasm for new technological developments is to present a vision of the future which is no more than a bad infinity of gadgets and devices and one that leaves us feeling saturated, jaded and even apathetic. Like a junk cereal, it's unsustaining. *Only* snap, crackle and pop. We become, after a while, inoculated against any feelings of surprise or anticipation, so that the future comes to seem, paradoxically, *un*exciting.

Far more important, however, than all the image and hype of the *Tomorrow's World* rhetoric, is the way in which the programme *mystifies* our understanding of science and technology. Like a great deal of television output, *Tomorrow's World* connives in the myth of expertise and knowledge. It asks us to stand in awe at what scientists pull out of their top hats. It invites us to defer to a figure whose status and power (founded upon knowledge) is inverse to that of the viewer (founded upon ignorance). Significantly, however, the figure of the scientist is physically absent from the programme. Perhaps it is felt that his or her mandarin language will alienate the average peak-time viewer. Or perhaps it is assumed that he or she will be lacking in charisma. The consequence, though, is that the authority of the scientist (and of Science) is enhanced. Scientists become remote and revered deities above and beyond the daily run of things. Their expertise is safely protected from scrutiny and possible demystification. They, the seekers after truth and knowledge, are invoked in respectful and deferential terms. Thus, in the context of the energy crisis, 'Before oil dries up, scientists are quite naturally looking for alternatives.' And they seem to have things in hand. Whilst it took nature millions of years to create oil, 'incredible as it may seem, scientists have now found a way to speed the process up...' The transplanting of brain tissue? Well, 'Scientists have perfected a technique...' For them nothing is impossible. In our constant battle against the natural world, they are the champions of rationality and control. And servicing these Olympian figures is another kind of expert, the more worldly television presenter, the mediator of knowledge, the professional communicator who translates the hieroglyphics of science into colloquial language. The presenter is the 'user friendly' expert. He or she is the public relations expert, the sales rep. for the scientific, technological and industrial establishment. To him or her falls the task of giving the human touch to abstract and complex issues, of dressing up science and technology for public consumption.

The mystification of the role of the expert is, in fact, just part of a much broader mystification of science and technology in general. Far from illuminating the workings of science and technology, *Tomorrow's World* serves only to cloud our understanding and to obfuscate the real issues. When Roland Barthes says of myth that 'It purifies [things], it makes them innocent, it gives them a natural and eternal justification,' that it transforms history into nature, then what more powerful and resonant myth could be nominated than that which naturalises and neutralises science and technology? *Tomorrow's World* draws upon, and replenishes, a mythological orthodoxy – upheld both in the West and in the Eastern bloc countries – that places science essentially outside the world of politics and of ideologies.

In the discourse of *Tomorrow's World* science and technology are the panacaea for all social problems. The technological fix. So we have an energy crisis? Then the scientists will find techniques for the synthetic production of oil. No mention of why and how natural resources are being squandered and depleted. No reference to the debates current among ecologists. Stolen cheque and credit cards? Scientists can put a stop to embezzlement with the invention of a new device that registers our 'invisible signature'. No acknowledgement of the temptations of the consumer marketplace, nor of the problem of social inequalities. Politics is exorcised in favour of technological management.

For *Tomorrow's World*, science and technology are inherently neutral forces. They may be applied wisely or foolishly, but in themselves they are socially neutral. Immaculately conceived and pure, they stand outside and above the realm of the social. So powerful and insistent is this myth of neutrality, that a new device for linking advanced television cameras with an image processing computer for the purpose of motorway surveillance can be presented as simply another technical breakthrough by electronics experts. Will not the routine surveillance of motorway traffic benefit those who have had their cars stolen? Again, no mention of pre-emptive policing, nor of the civil liberties' implications of surveillance techniques.

Science and technology evolve in the laboratory – outside the social sphere. They have their own autonomy, momentum and inevitability, to which we must grow accustomed and adapt. Science has nothing to do with social choice and decision-making. For the most part its 'impact on society' – as if it were not itself an integral aspect of society – is beneficial. It gives us the infrastructure of our social life: from power stations to video games, from medical science and technology to communications satellites. And this we call 'progress'. Often it may throw up problems, for the road to the future is not all smooth. Thus the question of brain tissue transplants leaves us still with 'some ethical problems to sort out.' This, however, can be left in the capable hands of yet other experts – the philosophers and professional moralists of the Warnock Committee, for example, will seek to lay down guidelines on genetic engineering. (But what of the ethics of police surveillance or nuclear weapons?)

The achievement of this powerful myth – of this scientism – is to effectively depoliticise, dehistoricise and desocialise our understanding of science and technology. Repressed is any awareness of those forces that constitute the technologies to express their own narrow and particular values and priorities: nuclear corporations; pharmaceutical companies; electronics and aerospace interests; police and military agencies. No mention of transnational corporations, of capital and of profit making. No mention of the relations of power that in reality shape and inform the supposedly neutral realm of science and technology. Nowhere is it suggested that technology grinds people down in factories, that it leads to ecological devastation and pollution, or that it may now threaten even our very survival. Within this discursive realm, in Barthes's words, 'A conjuring trick has taken place: it has turned reality inside out, it has emptied it of history and has filled it with nature...'

Long before Barthes, Marx, too, saw that the ideologues of capitalist reality seek to turn the historical dynamic of capital accumulation 'into a supposed law of nature.' The consequence of this is that, for the mythologue, 'there has been history, but there is no longer any.' History and change dissolve into an eternal present. For all its futuristic rhetoric, *Tomorrow's World* remains thus frozen in a static and eternal present. It offers us not a real future, but an extension of the present. Tomorrow's world is the same as it is now. There is just more of it.

John O. Thompson

TV Magazines: Workers' Profiles?

Imagine that every week the *Radio Times* and the *TV Times* were much thicker than they now are; so thick that everyone who'd worked on that week's television could have his or her profile written up. Who would get profiled under these expansive circumstances who isn't profiled now? And would the profiles be written to the same plan?

In the *RT* and *TVT* as we know them, two criteria seem to be used to distinguish the profileable television workers from the rest. You can get your life and work discussed if you are in a position of *single authorship* with regard to a programme. Playwrights are central examples of this. But you can equally rate a reporter's attention if you are about to be *visible* on *RT/TVT*-readers' screens; and here the central examples are actors. It follows that if you are a performer generating your own material, you are doubly profileable; but either claim on the reader's attention will do.

Note that these criteria cut across the head-versus-hand divide. Management is, in general, as non-profileable as the canteen staff because management's relation to authorship isn't easy to grasp. Note also that the criteria don't necessarily coincide with narrative criteria. Maybe the slog of film-editing on *The Sweeney* isn't the stuff of which entertaining journalism is made. The life of a researcher, though, is rich in narrative potential (witness the researcher-heroine in the recent Northern Ireland film shown on Channel Four, *Acceptable Levels*). Yet the researcher isn't profileable, being neither visible nor able to be thought of as a simple (non-collaborative) point of origin for the visible.

An egalitarian, hence huge, *RT* or *TVT* would, in granting profileability to all, demystify presence (the visible) and origin (the authorial). But the thought of profiling the whole work-force brings out something else: just how strangely 'celebrity' workers are at present written up.

Imagine that the reporter is visiting, *not* Kate Jackson, ex-*Charlie's Angels*, now of *Scarecrow and Mrs. King*, but some other worker. Some other busy worker: the interview is all about work, the demands of work: ' "It's exhausting, absolutely exhausting," she says, pouring diet drinks, lowering Ella Fitzgerald on to the stereo, throwing the dogs out and finally flopping to rest on the sofa.' We are at home with the worker; we want to know what the work is like, what's exhausting and/or rewarding (' "If you're willing to pay the price the rewards are incredible" ') about the canteen or the van or the studio floor or the office. We are interested, are we not, in a professional life? 'Her professional life, if not her private life, is making her happy again.' Wouldn't we want to know about that happy-making thing, especially if (as 'she also admits') 'the pace at which she drives herself doesn't leave much time for a personal life'?

Apparently not: the reporter, on our behalf, is chatting, in this house that was 'meant to be a family home for her and her second husband and the children they talked of having,' about the imminent break-up of that marriage. *All* we hear of, where the professional life is concerned, is the pace, the pressure – up at 4.30 a.m. to fly to the studio – which crowds and sterilizes the private life. This worker, whose 'energy and confidence are phenomenal' – this Stakhanovite – is profileable over the issue of whether, at 36 and moving out of rather than into marriage, she may be getting too old to have a child.

This is an interesting-enough issue, and the mega-*RT/TVT*'s story-bank could presumably supply us with material in the same vein in each worker's case. But would it seem *natural* to profile the associate producer or the cameraman or the technical co-ordinator on *One Man and his Dog* so? (Or the secretary whose hours over a word-processor display screen may have induced a miscarriage?)

The *TV Times* profile of Kate Jackson being rather on the downmarket side, let us turn to *Radio Times* profiling National Theatre and Royal Shakespeare Company actress Cherie Lunghi 'in a week when she makes two more *appearances* on BBC TV.' We get a cover picture of Cherie Lunghi as herself, another full-page picture of her as Margaret in *Strangers and Brothers* and, on the page with the text, a picture of her as Sue in Howard Brenton's *Desert of Lies*. The piquancy of the coincidence of the double appearance gets heightened, not surprisingly, by the reporter's inviting her to talk about Sue, Margaret *and* Cherie. Here, as always in the discourse around acting, an endless prospect opens up for comparison and contrast, for expanding on the overlap, or lack of it, between Sue and Margaret, Sue and Cherie, Margaret and Cherie. Sue visits the Kalahari as a journalist; Cherie visits Africa to play Sue, and 'has no doubt about its capacity to change people.' (Confirmation of Sue's experience as authored by Brenton: a sort of co-authorship? Certainly co-validation.) Sue versus Margaret *vis-a-vis* Cherie: ' "There's perhaps more of myself in Margaret than in Sue... Margaret works from her vulnerability. As an actress, I have to do just that. Vulnerability is my main stock in trade."' Which last remark, minus the 'main', gets onto the magazine's cover. Cherie Lunghi (who, incidentally, clearly belongs amongst that proportion of television workers who would come across in the mega-*RT/TVT* as witty, intelligent and sensible) does, thus, in a way almost get to talk about her work. But the way the profile plays with the Cherie-Margaret equation has the effect of pulling the reader away from Cherie Lunghi's work towards her being. Cherie Lunghi is on the brink of telling us how she 'does' vulnerability. But when *Margaret* 'works from her vulnerability,' that means that Margaret (as authored by a chain, from C. P. Snow through the adaptors, the director and Cherie Lunghi herself, so complicated that the profile leaves the authorship unspecified) *is* vulnerable. So we don't hear about how one succeeds in conveying vulnerability if one is the actress Cherie Lunghi; for that question another is substituted: *is* Cherie, the real Cherie, vulnerable? 'Cherie Lunghi does not appear the least bit vulnerable. But if she says she is, it's impossible to believe anything else.' Conclusion of article. (*Has* CL said she is? Her work, being believable...)

All this, of course, is paradox-of-the-actor material (Diderot: actors must not be what they seem if the success of the feigning is to be kept under their control; Stanislavsky: yes, they must, somehow). But the elusive, depressing thing about the life-art parallel-drawing here is its reductive quality. Again, let us imagine how the following details would read if they were part of a mega-*RT* profile of a worker who was not an actress. Cherie Lunghi is presented as active and forceful, and as having a politics. 'Her future,' she says, 'will be modelled on the likes of Jane Fonda, who go out and create their own opportunities.' She is an active member of CND. But all this activity is framed so as to collapse it back into the personal, the public-personal of the minor celebrity. 'She is equally outspoken about political issues and her own private life. For five years Cherie has loved the same man, but has repeatedly declared in public that she prefers to live on her own.' (Film editor repeatedly declares? Personnel officer repeatedly declares? Van driver repeatedly declares? Jim Hiley, *Radio Times* journalist, repeatedly declares?) 'Now she explains... "I still don't attach any importance to marriage. I'm beginning to think about children, and that might lead me to feel differently in time." It is partly her concern for children that led her to the Campaign for Nuclear Disarmament.'

Partly – but that is the part, the only part, of the politics that will get described: the 'human' part, the womanly part. 'Until very recently, Cherie Lunghi claims, she failed to recognise how important appearances could be in an actress's career... "But now I'm learning

to assume a little vanity, to make the most of looks and glamour." '
So the profile begins, with what is overtly a work point but is bound
to be heard as Lunghi expressing a willingness to assume a proper
femininity across the board. So it does not surprise us that the
journalist's choice of a first illustration of CL's 'memorable turns of
phrase' should be this: ' "Developing a role is like a pregnancy," she
once announced.' The work, the enterprise, the politics, all get
written up within the standard womanly personal framework – looks
and glamour, love, vulnerability, children.

Meanwhile, the article having come to an end, another worker
gets seven lines to fill the page. '*Desert of Lies* and next Tuesday's
Hard Feelings are part of a season of *Plays for Today* produced by
Michael Wearing, whose award-winning work includes *The History
Man* and *Boys from the Blackstuff*.' Just that: no profile, no
photograph, no chance to talk about the work – but also no
patronising 'humanisation', no assumption that Michael Wearing's
family, or lack of it, is any concern of ours. Which is only natural for a
producer, rather than an actor, and a man, rather than a woman.

References:

Leslie Salisbury, 'Why I would love a family by Kate Jackson', *TV Times*, 16–
22 June, 1984, 11–12.
Jim Hiley, 'Cherie's blossoming', *Radio Times*, 10–16 March, 1984, 4–5.

John Hartley

Out of Bounds: the Myth of Marginality

Television and parliamentary politics have a lot in common. To begin with, both are founded on the concept and practice of *representation*. Members of parliament are our elected representatives, the government represents the will of the people in action, and various groups make representations to parliament. Television makes representations, too, though of a slightly different kind. It represents events, people, places, ideas.

Like parliament, the institutional organization of television is the adversarial, two-party system. The BBC and the ITV companies slug it out, getting progressively more like each other as they chase the same floating viewers. But occasionally there are crisis periods in both politics and broadcasting in which the marginal, grey areas between the two 'mighty opposites' takes on an apparently disproportionate significance. The two-party duopoly itself seems threatened by the 'minor' parties that occupy the ambiguous terrain around its edges: there is much talk of mould-breaking. In the event, the mould turns out to be surprisingly resistant to challenge, and the threat is contained in an institutional form that blunts its cutting edge. In the sixties, the ambiguous terrain between the two mighty opposites resulted in the Orpington Liberals, the Nationalists and BBC-2. In the eighties, the ambiguity is represented in the form of the SDP, Sianel Pedwar Cymru (S4C) and Channel Four. Oddly enough, the board of Channel Four is a hotbed of SDP activists, and its political ideology at Board level, while the commitment to pluralism and mould-breaking, not to mention the 'proportional' representation of 'minority' groups, is the same as the SDP's.

In parliamentary elections, as every television viewer knows, the focus of Election Specials on TV is not so much on the opposing parties themselves as on a different kind of opposition, namely that between *safe* and *marginal* seats. This is hardly surprising, since the difference between a Tory and a Labour government can turn on the distribution of a few hundred votes in 'key marginals'. These seats also provide clues about the shape of things to come – they are the signs that stand for the future. Here the boundary between parliament and television becomes truly ambiguous, since in an election there is no parliament, and the transition from old to new is ritualized by television. At the very moment when politics moves from normal executive and legislative safety to its risky, democratic margins, television takes over and distends the marginality of the occasion into a late-night orgy of suspense. In true soap-opera style, the outcome is endlessly deferred, and people's actions and decisions are endlessly discussed by the familiar cast of commentators and politicians. Throughout, the marginal seats are a constant focus of fascination for these representatives of TV and politics, because such seats magically 'prove' the rhetoric of democracy. They provide empirical evidence of the possibility of change within an overall structure that is not disrupted but vindicated by such change. In elections, then, the *marginal* is the site of change and development; the ritualized boundary between one State and another; and the opposite of *safe*.

So far it seems that margins appear, contradictorally, *both* as peripheries (the site of outsiders who 'don't count') *and* as zones of danger, where the security of 'safe' territory is threatened by what's going on at the edges. Once again, a parliamentary analogy will serve to clarify the implications of this. Both the major parties have groups which occupy their 'left' margins. In the case of the Tories these are the 'wets'. For much of the past decade the wets have been understood (in popular/media mythology) as irrelevant and peripheral – they don't count. For the Labour Party, however, there is the 'militant tendency' who have been understood (again in popular/ media mythology) as both threatening to the party as a whole, and even made up of 'outsiders' who have 'infiltrated' the party for their own purposes. Thus, from the 'centre' of each party, things that are going on at the edge can seem either irrelevant and peripheral, or disruptive and threatening.

It is obvious from this illustration that margins aren't 'naturally' one or the other. They have to be *made sense of* as either irrelevant or disruptive, and the way they are represented makes a lot of difference to our understanding. Think how we would view British politics if we were used to hearing about Edward Heath in terms of the rhetoric of 'militant tendencies', and about Tony Benn in terms of 'wetness'. But here a further problem arises, and it is one which applies to television. That is, the rhetoric which makes sense of a margin in terms of irrelevance may itself be the product of a *struggle*. In other words, if you can convince yourself and others that a potentially disruptive margin is, in fact, an irrelevant periphery, then any threat it poses to your security is thereby reduced. However, the more successful this strategy is, the more dangerous it becomes, since it encourages a *false* sense of security.

If we apply this idea to television, the most important lesson it teaches is that television *as a whole* has been represented in this way ever since it became the dominant popular medium. Even among radical critics, television has tended to be seen as less important, less worthy of serious attention, than other media (such as Literature, Cinema and the Press). It has attracted a few major theorists, either academic or political, and it is often dismissed as a 'bastard' medium, whose only interest lies in the way it debases both 'purer' forms *and* people's consciousness. Such attention as it does receive frequently looks at TV in terms of values and assumptions that come not from its own practices and regimes, but from more 'prestigious' areas of knowledge. Its genres are understood in terms of film, its politics in terms of the press, its values in terms of literature, and so on.

In short, television has been made sense of in terms that emphasise its 'wetness', as opposed to its 'militant tendencies'; so much so, in fact, that it is sometimes hard even to imagine that it has any radical or disruptive potential at all. Many radical critics of television, both within the organized Left (the Labour and Trade Union movement) and in progressive intellectual circles, tend to *dismiss* television as *marginal* to the main business of political endeavour. Thus, apart from ritual condemnation at annual conferences, the organized Left has no policy concerning television at all. It hasn't got beyond the nineteen century notion of a *newspaper* to represent its alternative point of view. And although there are many studies of how television misrepresents certain groups, ideologies and points of view more or less systematically, the 'disorganized' (academic) Left hasn't succeeded in showing how interventions may be made in mainstream practices to *change* these things. TV producers are preoccupied with issues that the critics have hardly begun to address – issues of populism, appeal and pleasure in a fragmented and disunited society. There is little hope of influencing them to change their ways whilst the criticisms come from a standpoint which simply doesn't take television seriously on its own terms. Far too much effort is expended on 'exposing' TV's (inevitable) capitalist tendencies, on showing how it 'mythologizes' or 'naturalizes' the values of a capitalist system that it is both a product and representative of. But not enough effort is expended on exposing just how much the habit of mythologizing belongs to 'critical' thinking itself. Thus, 'critical' thinking that represents television as irrelevant or marginal to the central issues of modern politics is not critical at all, but *mythical*. It provides a false sense of security for the critics who can point to TV's inadequacies without inspecting their own. But it is dangerous thinking, because it encourages ignorance – it encourages us to ignore television's potential for disrupting and threatening the very system it seems so 'naturally' to represent.

This, then, is what I mean by the *Myth of Marginality*. It is that kind of thinking which makes sense of margins as irrelevant and peripheral when they can equally be understood as disruptive and threatening. It is mythical thinking because it 'magically resolves' the ambiguity of marginality. It simply 'understands' that what happens at the edges either doesn't count or, worse, isn't there. So, the antidote to the myth of marginality is to look carefully at marginal, irrelevant areas for evidence of change and transition. Taking my critical cue from TV itself, I now want to look at its own practices to see how different kinds of boundaries are erected and transgressed, and how different marginalities act as disruptive agents of change, even whilst TV itself encourages us not to notice them. I have divided what follows into two classes of marginality: the *structural* and the *representational*. I shall look at each in turn.

The myth of marginality is doubtless given credence by the literary origin of the term itself. On paper, the margin is the edge of the page. Go past the edge, and you come to the brink. Go over the brink, and you fall off. This Flat Earth metaphor discourages a sense of margins as *relational* areas *between* two 'safety' zones. And broadcast television has no edges, only discontinuities between programmes. We are constantly being reminded by continuity announcers and Raymond Williams alike to see television as a *flow*. In this respect, the contents of whatever is broadcast *between* programmes (i.e., trailers, time-checks, announcements, advertisements, continuity itself) must constitute the principal *structural* marginality of television. Thus the myth comes into operation right away. We are encouraged to watch these marginal broadcasts (they have 'contents'), but to treat them as if they weren't there (they are structured as *gaps*). They're not mentioned in *TV Times* or *Radio Times*, or in audience research, and they occupy a timeless, not-television slot in the schedules. However, they are far from insignificant. The broadcasting corporations have recognized their inherent danger, which for them is loss of viewers, by turning continuity and trailers into a *genre*, with its own specialized production departments, its own conventions, and its own appeal and pleasure for the viewers. This genre, together with the nationalized margin of the closedown (in Wales we get *two* national anthems), is strongly marked and specific to television. It accounts for a significant proportion of annual broadcast hours. In 1982/3 the BBC broadcast 404 hours of continuity, or 4% of total output. This is comparable to minority programming, like news (4.5%), schools (4.2%), drama (4.2%), etc.* It is often technically innovative. Quantel, for instance, was first extensively exploited in Britain in trailers. More importantly, continuity and trailers establish channel identity, along with the most direct address to the viewer, and real time. In these ways they perform the important ideological function of naturalizing and giving concrete expression to the pleasure of watching television: the announcer's familiar face tells us what enjoyment *looks* like. And the trailers encourage the knitting together of our personal plans and those of the broadcasting corporation. We are positioned into relations of warm anticipation in the marginal non-space and non-time of in-between-programmes. And, sometimes, trailers are more pleasurable than the programmes they trail, since they can dispense with boring exposition and simply show the good (telegenic) bits, with the magic (how *do* they do it?) of Quantel thrown in.

This margin-genre is actually distending into programmes themselves. The title/credit sequences of, for instance, regular studio programmes are quite capable of costing as much as one whole episode of the show itself, and titles increasingly partake of the generic features of trailers. They also display an attribute of advertisements, namely frequent repetition of the promise of pleasures to come. But unlike trailers and ads., of course, these boundary sequences are structured not to take us *through*, but to take us *in*.

Beyond the marginal broadcasts produced by the corporations themselves, we come to the ultimate TV show, where you can see just how much power can be packed into a gap in the schedules. Yet in the myth of marginality, advertisements aren't there, either. Even though they finance it, they are presented as *supplementary* to the mainstream fare of broadcasting. Despite, or because of, their *populism*, they somehow don't count in 'serious' discussions of television's programmes, whilst their producers and the agencies that make them are normally neglected in 'critical' books about the history and practices of television production.

But advertisements are pacemakers for the consciousness industry. They are one of the most developed forms of capitalist production, since they promote consumption in general and in particular, whilst themselves producing a *non-material commodity*, individual consciousness. Along the way, they put 'safe' television to shame. They can be breathtakingly costly (a reputed £350,000 for the

* *BBC Annual Report and Handbook 1984*, BBC Publications, 1983, p. 130.

latest Levi jeans ad., with fourteen hours of footage shot, enough to make an epic feature film); they are formally and technically innovative; responsive to changes in cultural consciousness ('audience taste'); and, sometimes, outrageously honest about the relations of production. They tell us the blatant truth about capitalism.

A recent example of this is an ad. for Del Monte Orange Juice that has been carried for the last two seasons on Channel Four, made by the SJIP/BBDO Agency. In a Western/'Mexican' setting, the 'Juice-Man' travels in a black sedan to a village, where he decides whether or not to select the local oranges for Del Monte. When he nods approval, not only the 'Mexican' growers, but even the oranges themselves jump for joy. The landscape, music, faces, action and characters make up a world that is *independent* of any that we might inhabit, but it is nevertheless instantly recognizable. The stranger, a Man with No Name, has a marginal status in the village. He is an outsider. But he has power over what happens next, since the outcome of his intervention will decide whether the village is saved or destroyed. And his black sedan signifies a different kind of marginal disruption, that of the gangsters of Chicago. So although this *independent* world is fictional, and not one you could ever visit, it is real enough. And the relationships established in the strange landscape are real enough too. Another Western world – that of corporate power – meets the insecure, dependent (but loyal) Third World, and decides its fate with a nod of the head. The power of the corporation over the people who produce the goods is the device used to sell those goods. And the power of television to produce knowledge and consciousness, to make sense of the world, is used to represent that least marginal, most dangerous relation – between Capital and Labour – in the fictional guise of the Western, which is historically one of the most efficient vehicles for presenting actuality in mythic form. We don't need tuition in how to 'read' what's going on under the dusty surface of the fictional forms. It's a familiar language. All it takes is thirty seconds in the gap between programmes.

So much for the television that isn't there. But if we pursue the notion of marginality, and move from the so-called periphery into the 'safe', substantive areas of mainstream programming, we find that it persists. Here, however, marginality is not so much a *structural* 'gap' between discontinuities, as a *representational* marginality. In both fictional and factual output, it seems to be a by-product of television's commitment to realism. In soap operas, for instance, there's a commitment to representing family and community life realistically. But if you look at any long-running serial, it transpires that this very commitment drives the families and communities in question progressively towards the margin of what viewers might recognize as realistic. In both *Dallas* and *Coronation Street*, for example, first marriages are very rare (Hilda and Stan, Gail and Brian). The shows are peopled by widows, divorcees, remarriages and relationships that border on the incestuous (Lucy and Ray in *Dallas*). Children are uncommon, and where they occur their status is usually uncertain – marginal. Thus, the 'family' of Len and Rita Fairclough and Sharon *looked* like a 'real' family on screen, but the 'biography' of each of these characters would make scandalous reading in the Sunday papers, as indeed it did in the case of Deidre, Ken and Mike.

As for the communities of the serials, they are, despite the lack of children, *symbolic paedocracies* (i.e., ruled by child-like qualities, child-like preoccupations and actions). That is, the adult characters rarely engage in 'adult' practices (work, sex, politics, household management, watching TV). Instead, they are de-centred into adolescence: endless talk of self-discovery and personal relationships; endless looking for affection, love or esteem from others. Relationships are eroticized and gossiped about, but rarely sexualized. They are oral, communal, and leavened by play, banter, humorous put-downs and endless impending crises. Everyone is easily distracted from occupational tasks in order to talk, and whilst talk of *public* affairs and politics is rare and embarrassing, there's little sense of individual or even family *privacy*, either. And all of this, of course, is what inspires and sustains our desire to watch. The appeal of the serials is not their 'realism' as such (by itself realism would bore us to death) but the ever-more marginal aspects of family, community and personal life that are used to represent or symbolize it. Although they are committed to realism, serials are *driven* by representational marginality.

Similarly, the commitment to realism also drives television towards two different kinds of margin in actuality or news coverage. Mainstream news seems often to represent important issues by means of one of their marginal aspects but, by the same token, the important aspects of those issues are marginalized. An example (taken from ITN *News at Ten*, 25/10/82) is where the troubles in Northern Ireland are made sense of via their effect on the *families* of two kidnap/murder victims. So we hear about the men's children and family situations and about how many 'orphans' the event has left. We see a daughter of one of the men interviewed, against a domestic background, about her feelings. We also see inside one of the men's homes, as a bishop is filmed comforting the family. In this family context, the events themselves are literally senseless, and this is how they are described in the story. But, of course, there were other aspects to them, which were marginalized or ignored: the connection with Sinn Fein, sectarianism and the overall situation. Using a discourse of domesticity to make sense of that situation does not help to promote understanding of it among the 'family audience'. It only promotes understanding of the concept of the family which, in this case at least, is marginal to the event, so that from its point of view the situation in Northern Ireland *is* senseless. Thus, in general, there is a further attribute of the myth of marginality. The myth proclaims that whatever is on the news is important (when it is often marginal), whereas, conversely, it suggests that actuality coverage outside the news, especially late-night documentaries on Channel Four, and early-afternoon discussions on *Afternoon Plus*, for instance, are marginal (when they can often be important).

Marginal areas can, in fact, be so important that they attract extra special attention, and this takes us on to a different dimension of the concept. Instead of being *under*-valued as *peripheral*, some marginalities are *over*-valued as *dangerous*, ambiguous, even scandalous, and they become the locus of actual or metaphorical border patrols, frontier posts, barbed wire. Just as national boundaries are policed by vigilant troops, so are social and ideological boundaries policed by vigilante groups. Television is not exempt from *this* 'militant' tendency. Placing itself on the 'safe', commanding heights of consensual common sense, it *makes* sense of the surrounding terrain by seeking to construct clear, unambiguous boundaries between 'us' and 'them', between acceptable and unacceptable actions, beliefs and groups. But in order to sort out what should be inside from what should be beyond the pale, television *over-represents* the marginal, ambiguous, scandalous areas of society. Action series, drama, news and movies alike are founded on violence, murder and criminality; on deviance, dissidence and pathological behaviour; on illicit, over-displayed or 'abnormal' sexuality; on break-downs, break-ups and break-ins. These kinds of marginality, exploring the grey areas between black and white, serve both to define the norms that they are shown to be transgressing, and to *drive* television's productivity as a system for the production and circulation of knowledge and pleasure, or sense and consciousness.

Thus marginality can be both peripheral and dangerous, and television cannot do without it. But, equally, it cannot *control* the meanings that are produced in the process. For, in order to limit meanings, it must first produce *excess*. Television's signifying practices are necessarily contradictory. They are driven by marginalities whilst proclaiming their centrality. They are developed and changed in the peripheral gaps that they encourage us not to notice. And they produce more meaning than they can police. It follows that, no matter how strongly certain readings are 'preferred', television's signifying practices are more open to challenge than is sometimes thought. Even if television, like formal education, tends to work in the interests of the efficient development of capitalism, and despite its undoubted success in popularizing hegemonic consciousness, the fact remains that, like schooling, it produces more knowledge than such 'functions' require. And that knowledge is not under its control, either at the points of production, as we've seen, or at the points of consumption. Watching TV is 'relatively autonomous' from producers' and controllers' intentions and even from textual determinants.

And, to make matters worse for those who like to think of TV as a closed system of dominant ideology, another potentially risky margin has begun to threaten the security and discipline of the system in recent years. This is the margin between television and not-television, namely video. For TV audiences can now break up the carefully constructed schedule by time-shifting; can play around with naturalized images by using the freeze, creep and search facilities; can even re-edit and dub ('scratch videos'). It isn't exactly the mass appropriation of the means of production and neither are the two more organized uses of video beyond TV – pop and community video. But all of these are further evidence of how television *practices* escape the *intentions* of controllers and the *notice* of critics. Such practices mark a further moment both in the fragmentation of television and in the growing confidence and power of its viewers. Critics who bewail TV's ideological closure can only sustain their argument by ignoring or dismissing these marginal developments, when they should be using them as the basis for challenge, change and development in the social means of sense-making.

This brings us back to the connections between TV and parliament. For even radical critics of television seem to have been taken in by the myth of marginality. The *political* policy that results is no more than a pale reflection of the *parliamentary* model. In other words, their response to television's *dis*proportionate representation of marginal characters is to demand *proportional* representation for everyone else. Furthermore, these demands are directed at the 'safe', mainstream areas of news and entertainment, whilst the margins I have been discussing are largely left to their own devices. In short, radical criticism of TV hasn't got far beyond a policy of *parliamentarianism* to solve the problems of 'minority' representation. The result to date has been a kind of television version of the SDP. Adversarial opposition is rendered into a harmless and not very appealing alternative fragment (so-called minority programming) which is dangerous only to the viewing figures.

But the final irony is that even such interventions as these are rare, and are initiated more often by innovative professionals than by the organized Left, or cultural progressives, who think a lot about the 'politics of signification'. The latter groups, who claim to be in the vanguard of organizing counter-hegemonic consciousness, have swallowed the myth of marginality to such an extent that *collectively* (though with notable individual exceptions) they treat television *as a whole* as a marginal supplement to modern society – dangerous but peripheral. Their political energies and creative efforts are directed elsewhere, to the nostalgic safety of print, cinema, performance or 'live' (but socially dead) media. Meanwhile, because there's not enough organized critical discourse to account *for* them, and because there's not enough organized policy to bring them *to* account, both capitalism and popular consciousness continue to develop and change *unaccountably* in the margins of television.

© John Hartley

Ed Buscombe

Disembodied Voices & Familiar Faces: Television Continuity

Even the most repressive dictatorships in the world have not yet (*pace* George Orwell) attempted to force their citizens to watch television. It remains something we choose to watch, an indulgence, even if one of those luxuries we cannot now do without. Children are punished by having its pleasures denied. Only those who write about it feel an obligation to watch (and perhaps those who make programmes – though whether they watch anything but their own shows is not always evident).

For this reason every television service must be nice to its viewers. Not only must it provide agreeable programmes; television must also engage its audience, tempt them with the promise of good things to come. It is often said that watching television is a habit (usually, it is implied, a bad habit). But this is doubtful. Simply watching the flickering screen, irrespective of the contents of the image, surely holds few attractions. It is true that after every technicians' strike interrupting the service, stories circulate that a significant percentage of the population has continued watching, even though only a test card was being transmitted. But these stories are only ever told about others. No one ever actually admits that they were among those staring blankly back at the little girl whose picture the BBC shows when there are no programmes.

So perhaps the mere activity of watching is not automatically continued. Television is not really a drug, though it is often called so. Viewers do not simply want the same experience in the same way as the cigarette smoker wants it, even to the point where a different brand cannot provide exactly the right satisfaction. What the watcher of television requires is a continual stream of new experiences – even if they must all be recognisable as authentic television.

A television service must, therefore, constantly seek to allure its audience, to ingratiate itself, in order to persuade that it can indeed provide the endlessly renewable novelty which is craved. The programmes themselves are not a sufficient guarantee that the next day's offerings will attract us, because the present performance of an institution can never be a proof against future disappointment. Thus comes about the need to promote what is coming next. In Britain the

BBC has now for nearly 50 years held out against selling time to others to advertise their wares (though for how much longer?). But it devotes increasing time during the gaps it creates between programmes to the transmission of sequences designed to persuade the audience that it wants to watch tomorrow night, and the night after, too. And not only time, but resources; promos, as they are called in the trade (following the practice of making everything safe and cuddly by the use of a diminutive) were one of the first television genres to use the expensive new Quantel technology, which permitted split screen and other effects at the touch of a button. Indeed, so sophisticated are the means now employed to 'puff' the programmes that there is a danger of a lack of fit between them and the programmes they advertise, still often pinned to the essentially nineteenth-century technology of cinematographic film.

The increased slickness and budgets devoted to promoting programmes undoubtedly results in large part from the ratings war between the BBC and ITV. And, just as in the arms' race between the superpowers, any short-term advantage is almost immediately cancelled out by the other, with the result that only the arms manufacturers derive permanent benefit; so in the ratings war, in which neither side can afford to be for long bested by the other, only those who sell the new machine which will give an edge over the competition gain real security.

As has been often said, in such contests the two sides grow increasingly like each other, and it could certainly be argued that in the years since the founding of ITV the BBC has become much more similar to its rival than the old pre-1955 BBC. Yet in one respect there is still a small, but significant, difference to be observed, and it lies in just this area of activity, in the on-screen promotion of forthcoming attractions. The difference is simply this: the announcers whom ITV employs to inform the audience of its future programmes usually appear on screen, in vision and making direct eye contact with the viewer. The announcers of the BBC are heard, but never seen.

It is just because the difference is so slight, yet so absolute, that it seems to demand explanation. The bigger differences, after all, as for example that the BBC carries no commercial advertising, or that ITV has not so much sport or documentary, are familiar, recognised and easily enough ascribed to the economic and institutional differences between the two services. But such an apparently trivial distinction in such a marginal area (after all, we are not even talking about the programmes), and yet such an unmistakable variation in practice, surely needs some accounting for. If it were only a matter of degree, such as that ITV announcers were often in vision and those of the BBC rarely, then perhaps one might accept that the reasons were merely contingent. But that the BBC *never* allows its announcers on screen is an instance of that difference which structural linguistics insists is the foundation of meaning.

How to interpret this difference? The BBC's disembodied voice is, one might say, representative of a culture which puts its faith in the word. Television, we are often told, is a visual medium, but when the BBC wishes to address us directly it does so by means of the word alone. This is the voice of authority, speaking in the tones of Standard English which signal not only a particular cultural authority, but also a particular class, that class which has appropriated to itself the right to define what is true culture, what is best, and the best for us. In these tones we hear the authentic note of the public service ethos, secure in a belief in its own virtue and necessity. It is, of course, a literary culture, not in the sense that literature belongs inherently to this class but in the sense that what counts as literature is defined by this class. And what counts as culture generally; Britain, unlike the rest of Europe, has never accepted the cinema as an art form.

By contrast, ITV addresses us personally, in the flesh. Instead of the austerity of the word we are given the warm humanity of real people. And instead of the impersonal righteousness of public service we are seduced by the smile of consumer capitalism. ITV, after all, must sell us something if it is to live. Some *thing*. Its best chance is to lead us to those things through people. And the people it shows are just like ourselves. Whereas the BBC claims to speak for all by speaking in the tones of the class that represents the Good of the Nation, ITV speaks in the popular idiom. Its regional structure, not a single metropolitan body, but a loose federation of 15 locally-based companies, permits that its accents are those of its supposed roots in the places where real people live. And its representatives are 'personalities', known to millions, identified by name. BBC announcers are never identified.

Another difference: the BBC's announcers are invariably male; ITV uses men and women in roughly equal proportions. This is consistent with the BBC's evident desire to give itself authority. By contrast, ITV is more humanised, not the spokesman for the nation, but a member of the family. Its announcers smile a lot (research shows that in mixed company women consistently smile more than men). But, just as there is a calculating side to ITV's more populist image of itself (ITV companies are not, either in their structure or their purpose, notably democratic organisations), so, too, its sexual equality combines with the exploitation of sexuality. Its announcers, when female, are invariably young and pretty.

As with anything, history can provide some explanations. The BBC began as a producer of radio programmes (in the beginning was the word). The commercial system began with television; only afterwards did it sprout radio stations. So the BBC's refusal (is it a conscious policy?) to put its announcers in vision may be explained as a legacy of its past as an exclusively spoken medium, just as its class position may be understood through its origins in a Victorian ideal of the public good, defined before the perfection of consumer capitalism. ITV, coming later and finding that ground already occupied, needed to find another mode of address. Sensing that the BBC, still, in the 1950s, trading on its wartime reputation as the expression of the national spirit, had failed to adjust to the political and cultural upheaval of 1945, ITV took its chance to give the public not what was good for it, but what it 'wanted'.

Or is there a simpler explanation? Would the BBC have to pay its announcers more if they became publicly visible, names known to the audience; as in Hollywood in the earliest days, the producers resisted naming their stars for fear of the economic power recognition would bring?

Whatever the reason, it's worth recording that in earlier days, when television was the Cinderella of the Corporation, the BBC did have announcers in vision, some of whom, such as Sylvia Peters, were more famous than those who performed in the programmes. Channel Four began with its announcers in camera, seated in front of what someone thought was the domestic decor its viewers would aspire to. Now they are heard but not seen. Are they trying to tell us something in Charlotte Street?

Kathy Myers

Television Previewers:
No Critical Comment

It's 4.30 in the afternoon and already the drinks trolley is out. We sit watching a new ITV crime series: a bunch of depressive hacks with careers caught somewhere between the fantasy of Fleet Street investigative journalism and the reality of a lifetime subbing the greyhound column of a regional newspaper. TV previewing is not a prestigious job. With few exceptions it demands little more than the ability accurately to summarise a press release, placing a recommendation at the bottom: good, fair, middling, bad. The weather report of the box.

The BBC Television Centre squats on Scrubs Lane, Shepherds Bush. Like Mervyn Peake's Ghormenghast it is built on seven levels. A strict hierarchical caste system with the bosses, programme makers and technicians layered like a cake. The basement contains the toilets, make-up room, storage units, tea trollies and, in B309, the previewers.

B309 is home for 10 Fleet Street hacks every Friday. They huddle in the cramped, airless room with curling napkin, sandwiches and a thermos of coffee. The schedule has been preordained from the second floor. A diet of *Play for Today*, *Tomorrow's World*, studio-bound interviews and quirky, inoffensive documentaries like *QED*. Nobody questions the schedule, although there is a time remembered in the collective B309 mythology when somebody asked for something different. The request was not met and the BBC, that Reithian bastion of good taste, responded by claiming that it was already familiar with what the public and, by extension, the previewer wanted to watch.

Days in B309 pass undisturbed. Some fall asleep, others lurch off to the bar. Some watch, glazed and stultified by the boredom of it all, their blank pads slipping off their laps. Jealous of their point of view, or panicked by their lack of it, critics do not discuss a programme's merits. There is no collusion. As the credits roll, they return with relief to the subject of their allotment.

B309 is bread-and-butter work for the previewer. Nocturnal by nature the previewer will also be found throughout the week in the basement of Central TV, Charlotte Street, and Granada, Golden Square. Long hours accompanied by a fridge full of Perrier, a lap full of video tapes and a note-book.

But life is not all basements, and the TV companies organise weekly bashes for the press. These cocktail-style celebrations accompany the launch of 'prestige' programmes: for example, the single play, a new TV series or an 'influential' documentary (the kind of programmes which TV companies get awards for). This discreet pecking order side-tracks 'low budget' units from the press's gaze. Education, community programme, religious or current affairs units rarely merit a launch. Unless, that is, a name is involved.

Jonathan Dimbleby is a name. For the launch of his four-part *American Dream* series for Yorkshire TV, BAFTA (British Academy of Film and Television Arts) was hired. This is a favourite venue for TV companies; selectly nestled in Piccadilly, indigo and dove-grey padded seats, discreet lighting, amber 'ambiance' toilets. Dimbleby was there. The production team was there. The press was there and, of course, a gaggle of waiters bearing aloft trays of tinkling drinks and petit fours.

Television, unlike the film or music business, believes that food, not drink, is the way to curry favour with a previewer's pen. The exception is the BBC who, to some extent, find the lavish display of hospitality vulgar, not to mention expensive. Drum-sticks, deep-fried salmon balls, caviar chequers and piped paprika egg: the food of the nouveau riche is to be found in LWT, Granada and Central. The BBC prefers cold lamb chops dipped in mint sauce, sandwiches and filled pastry boats. Channel Four, with its programming brief of 'Something for everybody', not to mention proximity to Charlotte Street's numerous delicatessens, prefers 'the exotic'. The press, now familiar with Channel Four's deep-fried turkey and cranberry sauce sweetmeats, has yet successfully to negotiate the peanuts crisply coated in sugar-free yoghourt. The BBC's resistance to preview 'excess' in catering is partly thrift and partly a calvinist belief that if the product's good, it'll sell itself. A window dressing of croissants, designed to put the press off the programme's scent, is something they'd rather leave to ITV.

Previewers and critics are not the same, although in one sense they are united by the act of 'criticism': the sieving and processing of a programme's content for the consumption of an audience. Previewing is the less prestigious occupation and most Fleet Street newspapers employ staff specifically for this function. These are the people who compile or annotate the day's TV listings, passing brief comment on a programme. As anonymous hacks, culled at some point in their inauspicious careers from provincial papers, they receive no by-line, as opposed to the critics, whose opinions are named and personalised. The list of such 'names' includes such notables as Julian Barnes for *The Observer*, Peter Fiddick and Nancy Banks-Smith for the *Guardian*, Chris Dunkley for the *Financial Times* and the ubiquitous Clive James.

City Limits, Time Out and the now-castrated *Sunday Times Supplement* (which has moved out of the field of TV criticism into a more general area of popular culture) are to some extent hybrids in the sense that they attempt to combine both the functions of previewing and criticism. Through reviews, previews and listings, these magazines have attempted to develop a culture of television criticism, a method of adding to the viewers' understanding of the mechanisms and effects of television. Fundamental to these magazines' approach is that the act of previewing is not 'innocent'. Writers for these columns try to illuminate the politics, industrial constraints and techniques at work behind the production of a programme and, in so doing, believe that they add to the viewer's understanding of television as a cultural force and as a form of domestic entertainment.

This approach is in marked contrast to the value system which sustains Fleet Street preview journalism. Fleet Street previewers have adopted the methodology more familiar within TV's own in-house journals, the *TV Times* and the *Radio Times*, insofar as they rarely pass comment on a programme. The Fleet Street previewer's job is often little more sophisticated than that of providing a programme's story outline, list of speakers, performers, etc. Directors and producers are, by and large, ignored, except in film and some drama previewing, where the TV previewer adopts the language of 'Film Studies', listing the auteur-writer, director, etc. Little more than warm-up acts, previewers tease the audience's attention without giving the game away; the conclusion, the story, the punchline. The belief is that to give that information would destroy the audience's interest in a programme. At best they will provide annotated information as to the genre of the programme: soap, play, sit-com, drama, chat show, documentary, etc.

In Fleet Street any dissection or analysis of the programmes is done after the event: Peter Fiddick, Nancy Banks-Smith and Clive James have made their names reviewing programmes already transmitted. In this context the programmes are often used as spring-boards to raise other issues: the Nancy Banks-Smith idiosyncratic head-to-typewriter diatribe, the Chris Dunkley Overview, or Peter Fiddick's 'industry, background and social comment' pieces. Of the

Fleet Street critics, Peter Fiddick and Chris Dunkley have perhaps done most to champion the cause of TV as an important cultural medium, in this sense elevating it to the status usually ascribed to art, theatre, literature or film. However, this elevation has been done while ignoring the bulk of TV's output. Rarely will the quality papers run a piece on sit-coms, light entertainment, quizzes, sports' coverage, USA imports: the bread-and-butter diet of TV, the stuff which the punters watch. The 'quality' papers are guilty of sustaining two mythologies central to television: first that 'quality' is necessarily a rare phenomenon and that (with Leavisite zeal) the role of the critic is to upgrade the nation's viewing habits.

The second mythology is that TV is not a visual medium. In this sense TV is treated quite differently from film, where the spectacle, the visual qualities of the artefact are emphasised. When writing about television, reference is made to the acting, the script, the journalistic scoop and the revelation or punch line, but never the lighting, editing or camerawork. The 'visual' quality of a programme is treated as secondary to the writing, the hook, the script or the story.

From the programme-makers' point of view the most prestigious areas of the industry to work in are those of the single play, drama, arts and documentary. These are programme genres which have hi-jacked their 'high culture' credentials from other mediums: the play from the stage, drama frequently from the novel, arts from the gallery and the documentary from investigative reporting in Fleet Street. This connection is also borne out by the individual careers of programme-makers. Many play directors cut their teeth on the stage, and TV documentaries are widely populated by ex-press journalists.

In terms of home broadcast, this kind of prestige programming, the kind for which awards are won and by which careers are made, is in the minority, accounting for no more than a tenth of TV's output. Mainstream television – quizzes, soaps and light entertainment – is, by and large, ignored by the previewers and despised by the industry's programme-makers. A form of class and cultural snobbery can be seen here simply in the extent to which the despised forms have their roots in the popular culture associated with the working-class. Quizzes and the like have their roots in radio, vaudeville and the music-hall; soap operas originated on the radio in the '30s as detergent commercials. It is only in recent years that this kind of TV has generated any kind of academic, political or intellectual interest. Now a number of media courses around the country run study sessions on 'popular' TV, but this is a relatively recent phenomenon and not one which has percolated down to the pens of Fleet Street, who still, by and large, ignore popular TV. The exception to this is when soap stars or quiz masters are interviewed as personalities, or appear in the gossip columns. This cult of the personality detracts from the actual form, substance and structure of popular TV. This creates a hiatus, a gulf between what the public watch and what the previewers (and, in this case, the reviewers) write about. Yet it is the despised forms of popular television which regularly pull audiences of between 10 and 17 million; by comparison, a documentary or arts programme, regularly the subject of critical attention, rarely pulls more than three million viewers. These tensions between high and popular forms of TV culture, support a fundamental TV mythology shared by the critics and the industry alike, that the medium (with notably aesthetic/cultural exceptions) is fundamentally a waste of time. Interestingly, both the political Left and Right have conspired with this image of TV as a destroyer, not a purveyor of culture. Thus, TV is blamed for any number of problems, as it is seen to threaten, to erode 'real' culture (which takes place outside of the home): theatre, cinema, political meetings, higher education, or whatever.

Caught in this cultural clash between competing visions of the industry, previewers have learned to despise their trade. If they're lucky, the programme summaries, which are in essence the guts of a previewer's job, will be supplemented by the odd chance to do a personality piece. Usually, with the division of labour as it is in Fleet Street, even this small cherry will often be snatched by the staff feature writers. Even 'issues arising from' controversial dramas, documentaries and arts programmes are not part of the previewer's domain. These 'opinion' pieces are usually produced by in-house review critics.

The history of press office bureaucracy is as important as the perspective individual previewers in creating the current climate of the TV culture. Over the last two years, the previewing industry has, to some extent, been shaken up by the arrival of C4. Originally boycotted and derided (as 'Channel Swore') the previewers felt no need to take the programme content too seriously. They just kept an eagle eye on the naughty words, bare bodies and amateurish-looking programmes. ITV, BBC and the previewers felt smug and safe. This tranquil and self-righteous adherence to a set of outmoded notions of what constitutes 'quality' TV didn't last. The critics started writing more reviews about the best of Channel Four. *City Limits*, *Time Out*, *The Financial Times*, *The Guardian* and the *Sunday Times Supplement* all came out in reserved support for the Channel's work. Inevitably 'different' programming, new visual devices, avant garde camera-work, the risk-taking *Eleventh Hour* slot, etc., demanded more work and more critical ability on the part of the previewer. A simple story summary was just not enough. This created a retrenchment. Most of the down-market Fleet Street dailies tried to pretend nothing had happened, a move which Channel Four as an institution didn't take lightly. In an enormous marketing drive, the Channel made every provision to get the preview press into the building and supported this with the production of sophisticated and informative press releases. This direct attempt at 'seduction' of the preview press was in marked distinction to the stand-offish attitude of the BBC.

The gulf between the BBC and C4 exists for quite specific, historical reasons. TV previewing is a relatively young industry, made possible by videotape. Prior to that, the TV industry did not have the resources, space or time continually to screen films for the press. The BBC press office has a history of servicing the internal machinery of Television Centre, and acting as a sorting office for actors, producers and journalists. Its primary function has been to sift inquiries and protect BBC staff both from Fleet Street and the public. This administrative inheritance still affects BBC press office policy. Understaffed and inefficient, they are resented and bullied by BBC producers anxious that their film should receive a press screening, and also harassed by previewers, eager to get a programme 'scoop' in front of the other Fleet Street hacks. As a concession, the BBC rigged up a one-day-a-week previewing session, into which a randomly selected number of programmes were shown to the press. Controversial programmes (especially the fields of documentary and comedy programming) tended to be excluded from these showings and this began to produce a bevy of late-night phone calls to journalists from BBC producers anxious to smuggle their programmes past the BBC press office and onto the domestic VCR of a previewer. This trade in programmes prior to transmission is strictly counter to BBC policy, which militates against the removal of BBC tapes from company property. Desperate ruses have included plain brown paper envelopes arriving in un-numbered taxis, being left in GPO sorting offices and arriving on the back of a motorcycle.

As it is, it's almost impossible to get hold of BBC programme details until the last minute. Low on preview facilities and competent press officers, TV previewers and those responsible for compiling selections in magazines have to rely on the arrival of the *Radio Times*. As the BBC is at pains to point out, the *Radio Times* is handed out at the BBC's discretion. In 1982 *Time Out* tried to run full weekly listings and the BBC came out fighting. The case has yet to be resolved and is still winding its way through The Department of Fair Trading. It brought to light not only the BBC's desire to control TV programme details, but also the significance of the revenue brought in by the duopoly of the *Radio Times* and the *TV Times*. The price paid by all magazines for *Time Out*'s attempt to break ranks was a stern reprimand to any who attempted to provide anything like full listings, and a temporary withdrawal of the previewers' bible, the *Radio Times*. Without this, it's impossible to ascertain when or where a programme is being transmitted, which all adds up to create the impression of the BBC press office as concierge, defender of the BBC bastion – as if publicity were somehow vulgar and disruptive to the good works master-minded by BBC programme makers.

Fortunately for the press and the public, this is not an attitude shared by ITV, precisely because of ITV's more direct dependence for its health and wealth on the patronage of viewers and advertisers. It needs all the publicity it can get. ITV companies employ upwardly mobile men and women who've got by on their brains, personalities and knowledge of the industry. ITV press officers do something unheard of in the BBC: they ring up the press and encourage them to preview programmes. ITV companies do their utmost to help the press, arranging facilities, tapes, food, interviews and, if need be, transport at the drop of a hat.

This 'bums on seats' approach to the press has affected the policy of C4, whose staff had, almost without exception, the advantage of not being culled from the BBC. The C4 press office is an exemplary version of what a TV publicity machine should be. Combining the enthusiasms of ITV with the political nous which C4 demanded, the press office worked hard from the outset to debunk the new Right's 'Channel Swore' image, through a ceaseless flow of well-orchestrated previews, press receptions and a supply of comprehensive information. Unlike the BBC press office, their ultimate aim is to put the press in contact with the programme-makers. This flurry of activity in C4 has done a lot to raise the profile of previewing. Magazines which previously ignored previews have started sending someone along, from the music press, through women's magazines, foreign publications and the style-mongers such as *The Face*, *Blitz* and *Stills*.

C4's insistence that TV is a culturally important medium has caught the Fleet Street hacks with their pants down. It has been a long time coming, but this is part of a welcome move towards a form of public discussion of television which treats the medium as a whole with the respect previously attributed to the stage and cinema. The blossoming of C4's *Right to Reply*, and the installation of *The Video Box* (which encourages direct response to programmes from the public and the press), is further evidence of the shift in this direction. We have to hope that C4's respect for its own product will continue to reinforce this welcome set of changes in the form and structure of TV criticism; and about time, too.

Contributors

Cary Bazalgette works in the Education Department of the British Film Institute.

Charlotte Brunsdon teaches Film Studies at the University of Warwick and is involved in Birmingham Film & Video Workshop.

Rosalind Brunt lectures in Communication Studies at Sheffield City Polytechnic, and co-edited *Feminism, Culture & Politics* (Lawrence & Wishart).

Ed Buscombe is general editor of publications at the British Film Institute, editor of *Football on Television* (BFI) and author (with Manuel Alvarado) of Hazell: the making of a TV Series (BFI).

Bruce Carson is a part-time lecturer in Media Studies at Goldsmiths' College, London, and in Film Studies in the extra-mural department of London University.

Ian Connell teaches Communication Studies at Lanchester Polytechnic and is a member of the editorial board of *Screen*.

John Corner lectures in Communication Studies at Liverpool University and is co-editor of *Communications Studies* (Edward Arnold).

Sean Cubitt is national organiser for the Society for Education in Film and Television.

Bob Ferguson is Head of Media Studies, Department of English & Media Studies, University of London, Institute of Education.

Robin Gutch is a BBC television producer.

John Hartley lectures in Human Communication at Murdoch University, Western Australia, is author of *Understanding News*, and is co-author of *Reading Television* and *Key Concepts in Communication* (Methuen).

Albert Hunt lectures at Bradford Polytechnic and is author of *Hopes for Great Happenings* and *The Language of Television* (Methuen).

Bill Lewis teaches Media Studies at the University of London, and at the University of Kent at Canterbury.

David Lusted is a Teacher Advisor for the Education Department of the British Film Institute.

Len Masterman lectures in Education at Nottingham University and is author of *Teaching about Television* (Macmillan).

Colin McArthur recently retired from the British Film Institute's Distribution Division, is the author of *Dialectic! Left Film Criticism from Tribune* (Key Texts, 1982), and contributing editor of *Scotch Reels: Scotland in Cinema & TV* (BFI, 1982).

Kathy Myers, formerly editor of *Camerawork*, is a freelance journalist, and is editor of the TV section of *City Limits*.

Richard Paterson is Television Projects Officer at the British Film Institute.

Kevin Robins lectures in the Department of Languages and Culture at Sunderland Polytechnic, and is author (with Frank Webster) of *Information Technology: A Luddite Analysis*, Ablex Publishing, New Jersey (in press, 1985).

John O. Thompson lectures in Communication Studies at Liverpool University and is author of *Monty Python: Complete and Utter Theory of the Grotesque* (BFI).

Philip Simpson works in the Education Department at the British Film Institute.

Frank Webster lectures in Social Studies at Oxford Polytechnic and is author of *The New Photography*.

David Widgery is a general practitioner, journalist and author. He is a founder member of the Tigerstripe Association who, with Chatto & Windus, publish his next book, *Beating Time*, in 1985.

Elizabeth Wilson lectures at the Polytechnic of North London and is author of *Mirror Images*, and of a forthcoming book *Defiant Dress*.

Other titles from Comedia

No. 23 **COMMUNITY, ART AND THE STATE — storming the citadels**
by Owen Kelly
paperback £3.95 hardback £10.50

No. 22 **READING BY NUMBERS — contemporary publishing and
popular fiction**
by Ken Worpole
paperback £3.95 hardback £10.50

No. 21 **INTERNATIONAL IMAGE MARKETS — in search of an
alternative perspective**
by Armand Mattelart, Michele Mattelart and Xavier Delcourt
paperback £4.95 hardback £12.00

No. 20 **SHUT UP AND LISTEN: Women and local radio —
a view from the inside**
by Helen Baehr and Michele Ryan
paperback only £1.95

No. 19 **THE BRITISH MEDIA: a guide for 'O' and 'A' level students**
by Moyra Grant
paperback only £1.25

No. 18 **PRESS, RADIO AND TELEVISION — An introduction
to the media**
edited by David Morley and Brian Whitaker
paperback only £1.80
published jointly with the Workers Educational Association

No. 17 **NINETEEN EIGHTY-FOUR IN 1984: Autonomy, Control
and Communication**
edited by Crispin Aubrey and Paul Chilton
paperback £3.95 hardback £10.50

No. 16 **TELEVISING 'TERRORISM': Political violence in Popular culture**
by Philip Schlesinger, Graham Murdock and Philip Elliott
paperback £4.95 hardback £12.00

No. 15 **CAPITAL: Local Radio and Private Profit**
by Local Radio Workshop
paperback £3.95 hardback £10.50

No. 14 **NOTHING LOCAL ABOUT IT: London's local radio**
by Local Radio Workshop
paperback £3.95 hardback £10.50

No. 13 **MICROCHIPS WITH EVERYTHING: The consequences of information technology**
edited by Paul Sieghart
paperback £3.50 hardback £9.50
Published jointly with the Institute of Contemporary Arts

No. 12 **THE WORLD WIRED UP — Unscrambling the new communications puzzle**
by Brian Murphy
paperback £3.50 hardback £9.50

No. 11 **WHAT'S THIS CHANNEL FO(U)R? An alternative report**
edited by Simon Blanchard and David Morley
paperback £3.50 hardback £9.50

No. 10 **IT AIN'T HALF RACIST, MUM — Fighting racism in the media**
edited by Phil Cohen
paperback £2.50 hardback £7.50
Published jointly with the Campaign Against Racism in the Media

No. 9 **NUKESPEAK — The media and the bomb**
edited by Crispin Aubrey
paperback £2.50 hardback £7.50

No. 8 **NOT THE BBC/IBA — The case for community radio**
by Simon Partridge
paperback £1.95 hardback £5.00

No. 7 **CHANGING THE WORD — The printing industry in transition**
by Alan Marshall
paperback £3.50 hardback £9.50

No. 6 **THE REPUBLIC OF LETTERS — Working class writing and local publishing**
edited by David Morley and Ken Worpole
paperback £3.95 hardback £8.50

No. 5 **NEWS LTD — Why you can't read all about it**
by Brian Wheeler
paperback £3.25 hardback £9.50

No. 4 **ROLLING OUR OWN — Women as printers, publishers and distributors**
by Eileen Cadman, Gail Chester, Agnes Pivot
paperback £2.25 hardback £7.50

No. 3   **THE OTHER SECRET SERVICE — Press distribution and press censorship**
by Liz Cooper, Charles Landry, Dave Berry
paperback only £1.00

No. 2.   **WHERE IS THE OTHER NEWS — The news trade and the radical press**
by Dave Berry, Liz Cooper, Charles Landry
paperback £2.25

No. 1   **HERE IS THE OTHER NEWS — Challenges to the local commercial press**
by Crispin Aubrey, Charles Landry, David Morley
hardback only £3.50